# The
# International
# Encyclopedia of
# Horses and Ponies

# The International Encyclopedia of Horses and Ponies

## Jane Kidd
### Consulting Editor

Howell Book House
*New York*

Howell Book House
MACMILLAN PUBLISHING, USA
15 Columbus Circle
New York, NY 10023

Library of Congress Cataloging-in-Publication Data

The international encyclopedia of horses and
ponies/Jane Kidd, consulting editor.
p. cm.
Includes index.
ISBN 0-87605-999-X


1. Horse breeds – Encyclopedias.  2. Horses – Encyclopedias.
3. Ponies - Encyclopedias. I. Kidd, Jane.

SF291.I56  1995   94-35533
636.1-dc20    CIP

Printed in Hong Kong

10  9  8  7  6  5  4  3  2  1

# Contents

# 1 How It All Began

# Evolution of the horse

In modern times, it is possible to get the type of pony you want by breeding and cross-breeding. But, long before man was aware of the horse, it was changing and developing: these changes – evolution – enabled the horse to survive.

### From fox to thoroughbred

Seventy million years ago, the horse was only about the size of a fox. A vegetarian, it browsed the plants and low-growing shrubs of swampy prehistoric woodland. But, as the threat from meat-eating predators grew, and other animals fought for the limited space available, horses found greater safety roaming the plains. Here they had to adapt to the new environment – wide, open spaces and a diet of grass.

They developed greater physical strength and the ability to outrun their enemies. At the same time, their teeth evolved to graze more efficiently and so complete the horse's 'survival kit'.

### Growth chart

Thanks to a remarkably complete fossil record of the evolution of the horse, scientists can chart its gradual change into the ancestor of today's native breeds:

**Size:** The horse became larger and stronger.

**Legs and feet:** These became longer and there was a reduction in the number of toes, with only the middle one surviving. This last toe finally became the horse's hoof.

**Back:** The back straightened and became much less flexible.

**Teeth:** The incisor teeth became wider and some premolars developed into proper molars more suitable for grazing.

**Head:** The front of the skull and lower jaw became deeper to accommodate the increasing height of the cheek teeth.

**Brain:** The horse's brain gradually increased in size and became more complicated in its working.

## How the horse changed

The earliest horse (*hyracotherium*) lived in swampy woodland and was a small, fox-sized browser. It had long, slender legs designed for speed. It also had three toes on its back feet and four toes on the front!

As the world around it changed, this little creature slowly grew larger, faster and better equipped for grazing dry grasses. Gradual development led first to a sheep-like animal (*mesohippus*) – with only three toes on its front feet – and then to one about the size of a modern-day Shetland pony (*merychippus*).

From this time on, it is much easier to recognize the features of the modern horse. Further changes, including the development of a solid, single hoof, helped increase its speed and strength (*pliohippus*) and then completed the evolution into *equus* – the forerunner of today's horse.

**Hyracotherium**
(about 70–60 million years ago)
This early ancestor of today's horse was only the size of a fox.

**Mesohippus**
(about 35–25 million years ago)
With longer legs and neck, the 'horse' was now sheep-sized.

**Merychippus**
(about 25–10 million years ago)
By this stage the horse was pony-sized and grazed on open plains.

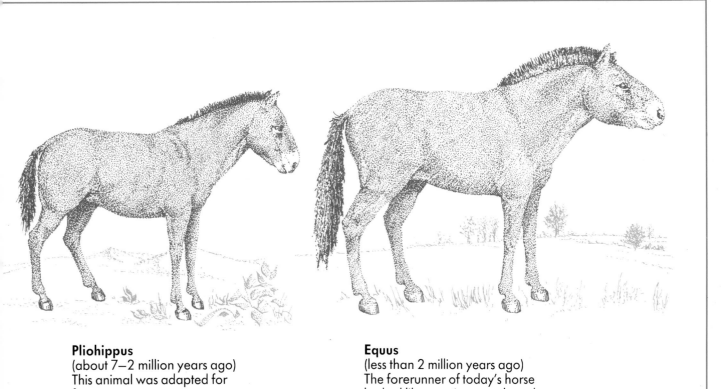

▲ **Przewalski's Horse,** the only truly wild breed still surviving to the present day, is closely related to the ancestors of domestic horses.

◄ **The first domestic horses** probably looked very like the now-extinct Tarpan. Horses resembling the Tarpan still live semi-wild – these are in a Polish reserve.

**Pliohippus**
(about 7–2 million years ago)
This animal was adapted for faster movement.

**Equus**
(less than 2 million years ago)
The forerunner of today's horse looked like a native pony breed.

# The horse family

As the last Ice Age came to an end some 10,000 years ago, much of the world was open grassland with isolated patches of scrub and small trees. Such land was home to large herds of grazing animals, including many different members of the horse family.

## The same name

Today, the horse has only a tiny handful of remaining family members – the wild ass (or donkey), its smaller relative the onager, and three distinct types of zebra – but, because they are so closely related, science has given them the common name *Equus*.

## A donkey's tale

The wild ass was once widespread in northern Africa, south-west Asia and parts of Arabia but very few still survive in their native environment.

The African branch of the family is distinguished by its grey coat, white belly and stylish black stripes on the legs. With large ears and a harsh bray, it clearly resembles its modern descen-

dant – the domestic donkey. It also shares many of the characteristics associated with the donkey: strength, stubbornness and a long life expectancy.

The smaller onager, from Asia, is sand-coloured, more lightly built and more like a horse in appearance. It has a much less amenable personality than its African cousin and has not, therefore, adapted well to domestication.

## Mix and match

Horses and asses do not inter-breed in the wild but, because they are so closely related, they have been cross-bred by man for many years. The result is an animal the size of a small horse but with more strength and stamina than either of its parents.

A cross between a male ass and a mare produces a mule. It has the head of a donkey and the tail of a horse. When a stallion is crossed with a female ass, the offspring is known as a hinny and has the head of a horse and the tail of a donkey.

Mules are much more common than

▼ **The African wild ass** is donkey-like in appearance but has stylish black leg markings. Sadly the species is now in danger of extinction: there are only a few hundred of them left in the world and their future may depend on the success of captive breeding programmes.

hinnies because they are easier to breed, but both are popular as work animals. Their only disadvantage is that they can very rarely produce offspring of their own.

## Stars with stripes

Of all the horse family, the plains zebra (or Quagga) can boast the most successful lifestyle. It still lives in vast herds that graze the grasslands of South and East Africa and provide a star attraction for visiting tourists 'on safari'.

There are, in fact, three distinct types of zebra – Grevy's zebra, the Mountain zebra and the Quagga. All are unique to Africa and all are characterized by their familiar black and white markings. The pattern of their stripes varies from one species to another and, within each species, there are sub-groups with yet more subtle variations. These are also slightly different from one individual to another so no two zebras have identical markings. The black and white stripes are an effective defence against the zebras' predators.

▲ **When a male donkey** is crossed with a mare, the offspring is known as a mule. It is the same size as a horse, but has a donkey-shaped head and a proverbially stubborn nature!

◄ **The domestic donkey** is a direct descendant of the African ass. Popular throughout the world as a beast of burden, this sturdy little animal seldom measures much more than 10 hands high.

► **The greatest success** story of the horse family is *Equus quagga* — the plains zebra. Some 200,000 continue to live in wild herds scattered across the dry grasslands of Africa.

**DID YOU KNOW?**
The plains zebra is also known as the Quagga — a name derived from the peculiar sound of its braying.

By contrast, the mountain zebra — a species which is on the brink of extinction — is thought to be completely silent!

★ **ZEBRA CROSSING**
The wonderful striped markings on the zebra provide a unique defence against predators. The animals stay in herds and group closely together whenever danger threatens.

The striped markings break up the outline of each animal and, as the herd runs away, small groups criss-cross with one another making it difficult for the predator to focus easily on any individual.

Their markings are so distinctive that this whole branch of the horse family is named after them.

# Unlikely relatives

## Evolution of horses' feet

4-toed; padded front foot

Toes reduced, from 4 to 3; central toe enlarged

Walked on central toe; lost pad

Side toes disappeared from view; solid, single hoof

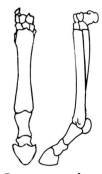

Forerunner of today's horse

There are two separate groups of animals with hooves and, surprisingly, they are distinguished from one another by the number of their toes! One group, which includes sheep and cows, has an even number of toes and the other – the horse's group – has an odd number.

## A common ancestor

All plant-eating animals have evolved from the same ancestors but, over millions of years, differences have emerged which now give us many species. The earliest plant eaters were all quite small – some no bigger than a dog. They moved on four legs, each foot had five toes and there was a 'hoof' (like a toe nail) on the end of each toe.

These animals, called 'ungulates', walked on the soles of their feet, with the toes pointing forward – just as humans do.

## Disappearing toes

As conditions around them changed, the early plant eaters were increasingly threatened by the early meat eaters and a good defence was to run faster. They learned to place their weight more on their toes, with their heels raised – again, as humans run today. Later still, they came to walk on the very tips of their toes – like a ballet dancer on 'points'.

When an animal balances this way, not all its toes reach the ground because some are shorter than others. This in turn means that the short toes are no longer of any use and so, gradually, they disappeared.

## Odd-toed ungulates

Today this group contains only the horses, tapirs and rhinoceroses – all the other species have died out. During the course of evolution the number of toes reduced to either three or one (the tapir has a fourth toe – but only on its front feet). The central toe bears the weight of the animal.

domestic horse

Malayan tapir

white rhino

At this point in evolution, seemingly small differences between the plant eaters led to major, long-term distinctions. All the plant-eating animals lost the shortest toe first. Some animals did not lose any other toes and to this day have an even four. Some had third and fourth toes of about the same length and these bore the weight of the animal between them. This meant that, as well as the first toe, the second and fifth disappeared leaving only two toes – another even number.

Others had a long third toe and second and fourth toes that were almost as long. They lost only the first and fifth toes, keeping three – an odd number. In horses, the legs and feet became more and more specialized for fast running, eventually leaving just an odd toe on each foot.

## *Rival groups*

For a time, the odd-toed animals were numerous and there were many different species. But, by about 37 million years ago, they were beginning to 'lose out' to the even-toed species. Apart from having different feet, the even-toed animals had also evolved more complex stomachs; as 'ruminants' they could digest food more efficiently and so survived more easily.

One by one, the odd-toed species died out and, today, the only survivors are the horse and its two unlikely looking relatives – the tapir and the rhinoceros.

## Even-toed ungulates

This group includes most of the world's large, plant-eating mammals, and all the cloven-hooved animals such as deer, sheep, camels, pigs and cows. They have two or four toes, the two central toes bearing the weight of the animal.

**red deer**

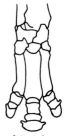

**Bactrian camel**

**domestic sheep**

### Ungulate forelegs

**The tapir** has 4 front toes and 3 hind toes

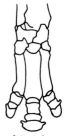

**The rhino** has 3 toes on each of his feet

**The deer** stands on the tips of its 2 middle toes

**The sheeps'** 2 toes give cloven (split) hooves

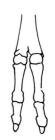

**Camels' feet** are broad for walking on sand

# Life history

The life expectancy of a domesticated horse is about 25 years – for a horse in the wild, it is slightly less. From birth to death, the horse's life is a series of milestones.

## Under threes

The horse is very well developed from the moment he enters the world. Within 24 hours of birth, a foal in the wild has to be able to gallop with the herd if he is to survive. For this reason, he has very long legs (nearly their adult length) and an instinct to get up and start moving as soon as he is born.

During his first month of life, a foal's height increases by about a third. By the end of his first year, he is three-quarters of his adult height.

After weaning, which happens at about six months old in domestication and slightly later in the wild, a youngster is called a weanling. On his first birthday, he becomes known as a yearling. After this, he is a two-year-old, a three-year-old, and so on.

A horse is broken in at about three years of age. Youngsters must be trained gently and gradually because stress can shorten their lives.

## Work begins

Most horses are fully mature at the age of six. If he is to have a long working life, a horse must not be put to hard work until he is fully mature.

▲ **Although they look out of proportion,** foals have long legs so that they can keep up with the herd from birth. A foal tries to stand up within minutes of being born, and can canter confidently alongside his mother when he is only a few days old.

► **Yearlings** are three-quarters of their adult height. They haven't quite filled out yet so they look rather lanky.

◄ **By the time a horse is three years old,** he has reached his adult size and is ready to begin his training. He learns to accept a rider through patient training on the lunge.

Racehorses reach their peak as three-year-olds. They are trained as two-year-olds and race for a couple of seasons before retiring and finding new jobs as riding horses or as sires for the next generation of racehorses.

Racehorses are different. They often work their hardest as three-year-olds. This is because a racehorse is not expected to have a long working life. At the age of four, the average racehorse retires to stud. If his career is cut short by injury before then, he is sometimes used to sire foals or finds new work as a riding horse if he is fit enough.

## Old age

A horse starts to grow old when he is about 15. From then on, his body systems work less efficiently than before. He loses his strength and finds he cannot work as hard as when he was young. But he is still good for many years, provided that he is given a suitable diet, has plenty of regular, gentle exercise and is well clothed and sheltered in winter.

Domesticated horses are rarely left to die in pain. They are put down rather than allowed to suffer. It is kindest if the vet comes to the horse while he is in his stable, so that he dies in familiar surroundings.

In the wild, horses die slightly younger than in domestication because life is harder with no veterinary attention and the threat of predators. When a horse senses that death is near, he may leave the herd to be on his own and die in peace.

▼ **As a horse grows older,** he slows down and finds it harder to do the tasks he used to be able to do easily. During old age a horse needs more care and attention from his owner to make sure he's comfortable.

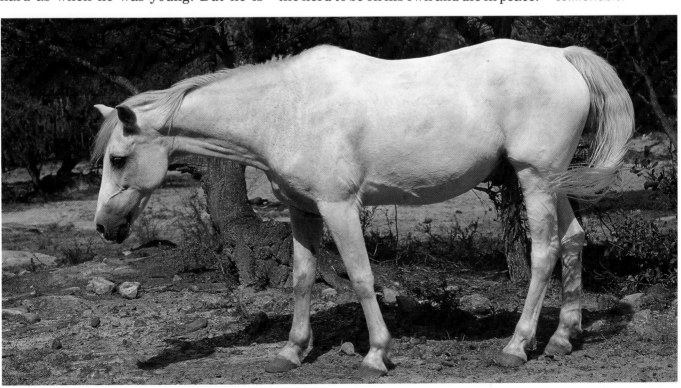

# The hot and cold-bloods

As herds of wild horses migrated to different parts of the world, they underwent changes to adapt to their new habitats. Variations in climate and food produced their own types of horse. The two extreme types were the cold-bloods and the hot-bloods, who had different appearances and temperaments. Modern-day breeds of horse have evolved from these and from cross-breeding.

## Cold-bloods

In the northern regions of the world, the climate produced lush pastures. The horses that lived there became heavy, strong and slow moving. To help them survive the freezing weather conditions in winter, nature equipped these horses with a thick skin and a layer of fat underneath it.

Most of the work and heavy draught horses of today fall into the category of cold-bloods. The biggest breed of cold-bloods (in fact the biggest breed in the world) is the British Shire. These horses can reach 17 or 18 hands high, and

▲ **The Ardennais** is a typical cold-blooded horse. Massive, powerful and tough, it can survive in the coldest and wettest weather.

► **Cold-blooded horses** adapted to life in the north. Today, they are strong but docile and make ideal workhorses.

weigh up to 1300kg (2900lbs) – the equivalent of 17 fully grown men!

## Hot-bloods

Hot-bloods developed quite differently from their northern relatives. In the south, where they lived, there were less extremes of climate. As a consequence, southern horses had thin coats to keep them cool and comfortable in the hottest of weather.

Food was in short supply, so the horses learned to survive from poor grazing. This also made them lighter, although they were still quite large. In their new habitat there were often few places for them to hide in times of trouble, so they became swift to escape their predators.

The Arab and Barb are well-known examples of the hot-bloods. The Arab is renowned for its courage, stamina and speed and has been much used for cross-breeding. The Barb has a reputation based on sure-footedness, strength and endurance.

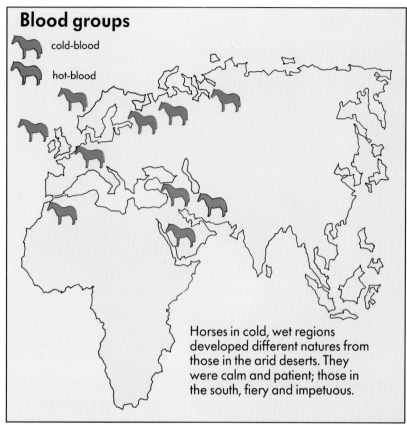

**Blood groups**

cold-blood

hot-blood

Horses in cold, wet regions developed different natures from those in the arid deserts. They were calm and patient; those in the south, fiery and impetuous.

▲ **The fine bone-structure** of the Tersky's head instantly betrays its hot-blooded origins.

► **Arab horses** have evolved to cope with harsh desert conditions and the constant threat of fatigue, hunger and thirst.

# The gene machine

The 'masterplan' of a foal's appearance and conformation comes from the genes he inherits from his parents. In domestic breeding, the choice of the right mare and stallion is, therefore, all-important.

## Passing on information

Inheriting particular looks or personality is all to do with 'genes'. Genes contain the information that makes every living thing the way it is – in a horse, they 'programme' whether it is, say, bay or dun; calm or high-spirited; athletic or clumsy. This information is passed on from one generation to the next.

Think of families you know. There are definite likenesses between sisters and brothers – they may all have a similar straight nose or blond hair. When you see their parents, you can tell where the resemblance comes from: they may have inherited features from their father and hair colour from their mother.

## Generation gap

Within that blond-haired family, however, there may be one who looks completely different and has, say, red hair. This is because some genes can 'skip' gener-

ations, and the red hair may have come originally from a grandparent.

The same goes for horses. A palomino stallion may be able to pass on his colour to his foals but, if he carries a chestnut gene from further back in his family, one or more of the foals could well be chestnut.

The information in genes also plays a part in programming characteristics of conformation and temperament. This can be used to 'plan' better foals. A long-backed mare and a short-backed stallion could produce a foal with the perfect length of back. But don't rely on two wrongs making a right: the foal could just as easily turn out with the same back fault as one of the parents.

## A bit of a gamble

You can never predict with absolute certainty what a foal will be like – breeding horses can be a real gamble. A foal can have pony-sized parents yet grow very tall, and grey parents may produce a dark chestnut foal.

But there are ways of lessening the gamble. High-quality stallions of known breeding are more likely to pass on their good points

to their foals. Combined with the best possible mares, the gamble becomes more likely to pay off.

## Combining breeds

There are many well-known breeds whose qualities are valued for cross-breeding all over the world.

The Arab is one of the most beautiful and ancient of breeds. They have been used for centuries to give elegance, endurance and spirit to top-class breeds.

The Thoroughbred, descended from the Arab, is a superb cross with practically any other type. Thoroughbreds add speed and agility.

Warmbloods are very popular as all-round sports horses for dressage, eventing and show jumping. Warmblooded breeds such as the Hanoverian, the Dutch Warmblood and the Trakehner are known as compound breeds – they are made by mixing Thoroughbreds and Arabs with local carriage horses.

Hardiness, cleverness and strength are all qualities found in the native pony breeds of Great Britain. They can make some very successful crosses – and many a Grand National winner has had a touch of pony blood.

►**Colour:** A foal may not necessarily take after its mother. It may inherit the colour of its coat from its father or even from a grandparent.

Some pure breeds can only be a specific colour but not so this New Forest mare and foal: they could have been anything except piebald or skewbald.

# Cross-breeding

| | Native | Draught | Warmblood | Thoroughbred | Arab |
|---|---|---|---|---|---|
| **Arab** | Can be a very good cross. High-quality riding ponies. | Definitely not – too much difference in type to make the cross worthwhile. | A good cross with the lighter Warm-bloods such as the Trakehner, but definitely not with the heavier breeds. | Anglo-Arab. Excellent all-round show and riding horses. A very popular cross. |  Pure-bred Arab. |
| **Thoroughbred** | A successful cross combining the good qualities of the two breeds. The foundation for many successful riding club horses, show jumpers and hunters. | A popular cross which produces strong horses such as show jumpers and hunters. | All warmblooded breeds make excellent crosses with Thoroughbreds. |  Pure-bred Thoroughbred. | |
| **Warmblood** | Could produce a useful hunter or riding club horse. However, it could be a poor cross because Warm-bloods are themselves a mixture of breeds, developed over a long period of time. | Sometimes used to produce a very heavyweight hunter. |  Warmblood. | | |
| **Draught** | No point in this cross. Danger of producing a useless animal. With certain breeds, could get a strong riding school horse, but very much a gamble. |  Draught. | | | |
| **Native** |  Native. | | | | |

## Types and breeds

The Suffolk Punch and Dartmoor are examples of draught and native breeds. Breeding Suffolk with Suffolk or Dartmoor with Dartmoor produces a pure-bred foal of quality and value. However, there is no point in crossing a Suffolk Punch with another draught-horse breed such as a Clydesdale or a Dartmoor with, say, an Exmoor. Cross-breeding two horses that are similar, but from different breeds, clouds the purity of the line and produces a foal that may be sweet but is of little value.

Sometimes breeds are crossed so often and so successfully that the resulting offspring become a breed in their own right. This is the case with the Anglo-Arab, a superb cross between the Thoroughbred and the Arab.

# Herd behaviour

Horses are social animals. In the wild, they live with their family and friends in closely knit groups. They keep each other company and protect each other from danger.

## Forming groups

Mare groups – which are usually led by a stallion – consist of about 12 horses. Within the group there is a clearly defined pecking order with status depending on age and strength. The lead stallion has complete control and no other horse in his group dares to challenge his authority. Each group also has a senior mare. The other mares and their foals complete the herd.

Stallions without mares, such as young colts and older horses past their prime, find companionship by grouping together. These groups are known as bachelor groups.

## On the move

Herds have regular patterns of movement between morning, afternoon and night.

There are also seasonal movements. For instance, horses may move to a certain part of the range searching for

▲ **Two rival stallions** challenge each other, fighting for dominance of a water hole in Wyoming.

▶ **Domestic horses** retain their strong instinct to remain in a herd. But each horse prefers to have its own distance of at least 1m (3ft) in front and behind.

grass in late autumn, and another area in early spring when the new grass comes through.

Movement is not necessarily initiated by the leader. A dominant mare often goes first and the others follow. The stallion acts as a herdsman, making sure no horse strays and protecting the group from danger.

If another herd approaches, the stallion always goes ahead of the group to challenge the rival leader. Fights between neighbouring stallions are quite common but seldom cause a bad injury.

Stallions attack with their forefeet, rearing up and striking out viciously at the rival. They also kick out with their hindfeet and sometimes bite.

## Keeping their distance

Just as different groups keep their distance from one another, so do the individuals within each group.

When grazing, horses like to keep several metres apart from one another. This gives them room to move quickly if they are startled by something from behind. If a horse or foal accidentally enters the territory of another, a horse often strikes out in defence.

▲ **A foal** rarely strays far from its mother. Even when grazing, the mare keeps a constant guard over her offspring, listening or watching to make sure it is safe and sound.

★ **NATURAL INSTINCTS**
In show-jumping competitions, horses sometimes 'nap' or try to return to the collecting ring where the other horses are waiting.

They want to return to the collecting ring because horses, as herd animals, have a natural instinct to return to or remain with their own kind.

# Breeding

► **A stallion** uses his sense of smell to test whether or not a mare is ready for mating. When she is, she gives off special scents called pheromones. To study these smells closely, the stallion traps them in his nose by curling his top lip over his nostrils – this is known as 'flehmen'.

▼ **In any herd of horses** only the dominant stallion can mate with the mares. Here he herds his team of mares away from rival males.

Watching a herd of wild horses during the breeding season can be fascinating – particularly if you know how stallions and mares show their attraction for each other.

In a wild herd there is one dominant stallion who has the right to mate with any mature mare. Females can start to breed from about the age of two and they may continue well into their 20's.

## The mating season

Horses naturally breed in spring. From late winter the increasing hours of daylight stimulate chemicals called hormones in the bodies of both mares and stallions. These hormones prepare the horses mentally and physically for breeding.

When mares are ready for mating, they give off special scents – called pheromones – from their flanks and

◄▲ **As a stallion woos a mare** he sniffs and nibbles her. If she isn't ready for mating, she might well kick so he takes care never to approach her from behind. If she is ready to mate, she pricks her ears and allows him to nuzzle her.

around their tails. The stallion can detect them from up to a mile away, and when he does pick up a mare's scent the courtship begins. A domesticated stallion acts in exactly the same way and the presence of a mare in season can make him difficult to control for a novice rider.

## Courtship

The stallion raises his head, opens his nostrils wide, pricks his ears and sniffs the air. He then walks toward the mare with his neck arched, head tossing and tail raised. He may circle her and follow her around squealing and nickering. Then he sniffs and nibbles her sides, flanks and around her tail. He curls his top lip over his nostrils to trap her smell in his nose.

An experienced stallion always approaches a mare from the side to avoid being kicked if she is not ready to mate. If she is ready, mating often takes place several times until the mare becomes pregnant or 'goes out of season'. When she is pregnant, a mare carries her foal for 11 months.

## Rival males

In the wild each male must know his place. The dominant stallion chases out of the herd any outsider trying to take over and any junior male able to mate. He herds his team of mares away from the other males, who often try to approach a mare when the dominant

stallion isn't looking. They even try to steal young mares to start herds of their own. If they are unsuccessful, young males often go around together in 'gangs'. Females, on the other hand, always like to stay in family groups.

Only the strongest, bravest and cleverest stallions win the right to mate – old, defeated stallions often lead solitary lives.

## Foaling time

To give foals the best start in life, nature works out the timing of their birth carefully. With the mating season in spring and an 11-month pregnancy, foals are usually born the following spring. The weather is warmer and the grass is growing.

If a foal is born too early, he can suffer badly from harsh weather. There may also be little grass around, which means his mother won't be able to provide enough milk for him.

If a foal is born too late, he may not survive the winter.

# Rare and extinct breeds: 1

Although there are many different types and breeds of horse and pony around the world, some have already disappeared for good, and others are gradually becoming very rare.

## Reasons for extinction

Extinct breeds are those which no longer exist. There are two reasons for their disappearance.

The Dales (right) and the Fell (below) are modern breeds which have an extinct ancestor – the Scottish Galloway. Both Mountain and Moorland breeds inherited the Galloway's strength and stamina and became more useful to man.

**Artificial selection:** Many horses are bred by man for a specific purpose. When man no longer needs these animals, breeding stops and the horses gradually die out. The Goonhilly, for example, was much used as a pack pony in Cornwall. With the coming of motorized transport in the 20th century, breeding of the Goonhilly stopped and these hardy ponies are now extinct.

**Natural selection:** This happened mostly in pre-historic times when the climate in parts of Europe changed rapidly. Some breeds were unable to adapt to the changes fast enough and died out.

## Founder members

Some breeds that are extinct today played an important part in the development of modern horses. The Scottish Galloway is one of them: found in the Scottish borders until the early 19th century, this pack pony was used as foundation stock for the Fell and the Dales.

It is also thought to have played a small part in the foundation of the Clydesdale. Breeding of the Galloway stopped when the new breeds were found to be more useful.

## Rare breeds

A rare breed is one which has very few survivors. The decline in numbers is usually caused by the breed becoming less popular to man.

Some rare breeds have been saved from extinction because new uses have been found for them. The Norwegian Nordland, for instance, was formerly used as a draught horse. Today it is used for competitions and disabled riding and is sometimes put to work on farms.

A few rare breeds survive because they are used to produce other types of horse. The Cleveland Bay, for example, is a good carriage horse in its own right, but today it is more likely to be crossed with a Thoroughbred to produce a quality hunter.

## To the rescue

The survival of rare breeds depends almost entirely on the work of breed societies. These enthusiasts encourage people to breed horses and to register them in the stud book, so that a record is kept of the pure-breds.

The Dales almost became extinct just after the Second World War because of the increase in motor transport. In 1955 there were only four registered ponies. The Dales breed society acted quickly in an attempt to increase the number of Dales ponies.

Non-registered but good quality mares were considered for breeding. If they were found to be suitable they were bred with registered stallions and their daughters were entered into the stud book. Breeding continued until the pure-bred form was reached and the Dales was safe from the threat of extinction.

▲ **The Cleveland Bay** was once popular as a carriage horse but today it is widely used as breeding stock for hunters.

▼ **Clydesdales** are thought to be related to the extinct Scottish Galloway. They continue to thrive thanks to enthusiasts.

▼ **The Norwegian Nordland** was saved from extinction by renewed interest. Nowadays, this hardy breed is popular for general riding.

# Rare and extinct breeds: 2

A horse or pony breed may become rare in its pure form if it is merged with others to develop new strains. When numbers of a breed dwindle, in-breeding often leads to a decline in quality, which can in turn lead to extinction.

## Modernization

The Hungarian Murakozi is a heavy-weight farm horse which once thrived but is now becoming extinct.

The Hungarians began a programme of breeding stronger, sturdier draught horses by crossing the Murakozi with imported Ardennais and Percherons. The Hungarian Heavy Horse is the result and this new breed has now succeeded the Murakozi. Despite attempts to upgrade the Murakozi itself, fewer and fewer are being bred successfully.

Another breed facing extinction is the Danish Knabstrup. This lightly built spotted horse was once seen in circuses all over the world. Nowadays, because riders are looking for horses with more substance, the Knabstrup is most often crossed with the sturdy Frederiksborg to produce more solid and versatile animals. As a result very few pure-bred Knabstrups are now left.

In the early years of the 20th century the Norfolk Trotter, also called the Norfolk Roadster, was thought to be extinct. Recently, however, some were discovered. This breed played an important role in the development of the Hackney Horse and influenced the French Trotter and Breton, the Russian Toric, and the Latvian Harness Horse. Few pure-bred Norfolk Roadsters now exist and the future of the breed does not look hopeful.

## New from old

The Russian Strelet is one breed that has disappeared. It was rather like a large Arab and was once used as a general purpose horse in the Ukraine. By the 1920s numbers were reduced to just two stallions and a few mares, and the breed was doomed.

With few sires and dams left there is little choice of mates so breeding is ▶

►The Russian Tersky is the result of cross-breeding the now extinct Strelet with pure Arabs. Breeders were anxious to pass on the Strelet's qualities of stamina and endurance before it died out.

◄The **Knabstrup** was once a common sight, but this lightly built horse is now in decline because modern-day riding demands more robust mounts.

▼The pure-bred **Murakozi** is becoming extinct because there is little demand for it.

bound to be between animals that are very closely related. When in-breeding occurs, any bad characteristics tend to appear in the offspring after a few generations. These defects may make the breed less useful to man or unable to survive in the wild, and often lead to it dying out altogether.

In response to the problem, Russian breeders sent the remaining Strelets to a stud, where the mares were mated with pure-bred Arabs and the stallions were put to cross-bred mares. The offspring of those crosses were then bred with each other. By the 1950s, the Tersky emerged – a new breed of good size and strong constitution. Meanwhile the Strelet in its pure form could not be preserved and the breed died out altogether.

◄▼**The Breton (left) and the French Trotter (below)** have a common ancestor – the Norfolk Roadster. While the numbers of the Breton and the Trotter are flourishing, the Norfolk Roadster is almost extinct.

## Rediscovery

The future looks rosy, however, for the Caspian which was rediscovered quite recently. This tiny horse inhabited the area around the Elburz mountains and the Caspian Sea, on the borders of Iran and the USSR.

The Caspian was thought to be extinct for over a thousand years. But in 1965 an American breeder discovered a bay stallion harnessed to a cart along the Caspian coast. Standing just 11 hands high, he was a perfect miniature horse of beautiful proportions, with a fine coat and a silky mane and tail.

The breeder recognized his quality and the importance of her find. For five years she searched around the Caspian sea as far as the Russian border for more miniature horses. In all she discovered about 35 of the breed, which she then transported to a stud in Tehran, Iran.

A careful breeding programme was started and some of the Caspians were bought by the Royal Horse Society of Iran to help ensure their survival. A new herd of Caspians was established and some of the stock were kept in natural surroundings on the Turkoman steppes. Unfortunately, many of these were killed by wolves. The rest of the herd was taken to safety immediately.

Seven mares and a stallion were flown to England, where a stud was started. This was a fortunate move because shortly afterwards, during the Iranian revolution, most of the breed remaining in their native land disappeared.

The future of the breed is now in the West. The British Caspian Society was formed and a stud book was started in the mid-1970s. A strict breeding programme was begun to ensure that the true Caspian continues to be registered.

The Caspian's calm, gentle nature and small size make it the ideal children's mount and driving horse. Recently several were exported to Australia and Europe. Although there is still only a comparatively small number of Caspians, enthusiasm from breeders makes their future seem assured.

▼ **The Caspian** was thought to have been extinct for over a thousand years, but this breed of miniature horse was rediscovered in 1965. Nowadays the breed survives mainly in Europe and Australia.

# Rare and extinct breeds: 3

One breed of horse, the Tarpan, is so rare that it can be seen only in zoos or in two special Polish reserves. Even more unusually, the Tarpan is technically extinct. Man's breeding experiments hold the key to the mystery.

### In decline

Before the Middle Ages, the Tarpan was common in forests throughout Europe. Slowly its numbers dwindled until, by the end of the 18th century, it had died out in the wild. Just a few examples survived in captivity in Poland.

Over the years, these horses were domesticated and cross bred. Although their descendants still bore a very strong resemblance to the original Tarpan, they became known as Koniks.

### The wild ones

The Tarpan was now officially classified as extinct, but interest in the breed hadn't died a death. In an attempt to re-create the Tarpan, Koniks were bred with Przewalski's Horses – the oldest and most primitive breed in the world.

▲ ►**Two rare breeds,** Przewalski's Horses (above) and the Konik (right) were mated to produce the modern-day Tarpan.

►**Modern-day Tarpans** roam free in government-owned reserves in Poland. They are almost indistinguishable from their primitive ancestors.

When Przewalski's Horse was discovered in Mongolia in the late 19th century it was as rare as the Tarpan had been in the early 18th century. Hunted by local tribesmen for meat, it was in grave danger of extinction.

A number of horses were transported to Europe, where a careful breeding programme was set up. Przewalski's Horse was saved just in the nick of time. Even better, breeding in captivity proved so successful that some horses could be sent back to their homeland in the mountains of Mongolia.

## A success story

Crossing the Konik with Przewalski's Horse was also highly successful. The new Tarpan closely resembled its wild, pure-bred ancestors – as much in temperament as in appearance. The Tarpan had been brought back from extinction.

## Breeds old and new

In the same way that man can revive an old breed, he can create new ones. When good-quality, elegant ponies were in short supply in Britain in the early 20th century, breeders set about developing a new breed.

Arabs and small Thoroughbreds were crossed with native Mountain and Moorland ponies. The result was the British Riding Pony – an excellent hack and leisure mount that fast become popular in Britain and Australia.

## In isolation

One breed that is in need of help from man is the Chincoteague. Inhabitants of the small islands of Chincoteague and Assateague off the east coast of the USA, these ponies have been unaffected by other breeds for hundreds of years. In common with other isolated communities of horses, much in-breeding has taken place – the Chincoteague's conformation is becoming increasingly small and poor as a result.

If nature is allowed to take its course, in-breeding will continue until the Chincoteague is unable to survive in the wild. New blood must be introduced to guarantee the breed's future.

**Overleaf:** The elegant British Riding Pony is a breed that was developed in recent years to meet the increased demand for good riding and showing ponies.

▼ **The Chincoteague** lives on remote islands off the coast of Maryland, in the USA. Isolated from other breeds for hundreds of years, it is dangerously in-bred.

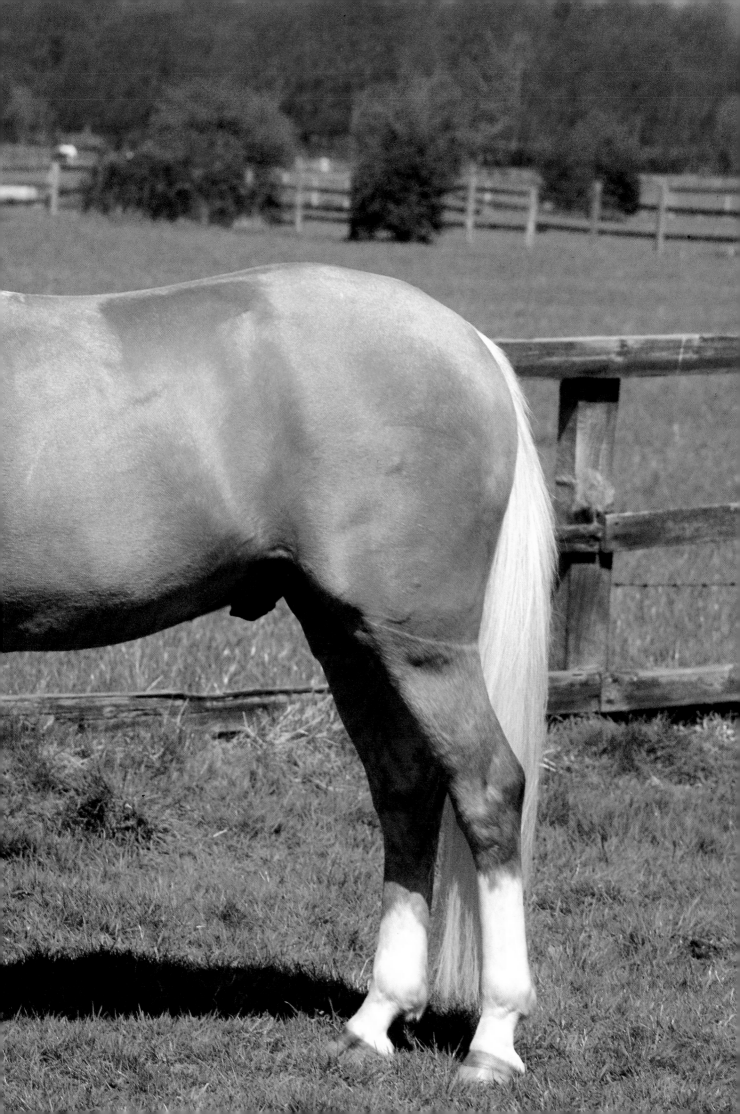

# Body colouring

The colour of a horse is determined by its coat, mane and tail. The main colours are bay, brown, chestnut, black, grey and dun, but there are many variations.

## Take your pick

No one colour is better than another, although many people have preferences. Napoleon, for instance, would only ever ride grey horses. Cowboys used to insist that duns alone had the stamina for cattle-herding, while North Africans consider white horses to be the noblest and blacks the most lucky.

As for coloured (piebald and skewbald) horses, they provoke mixed feelings. Associated with characters of disrepute in mediaeval England, they were – by contrast – very popular among American Indians. The Indians believed them to be magical and felt inspired with bravery when they rode coloured horses into battle.

chestnuts

browns

black

bay

cream

dappled grey

strawberry roan

blue roan

spotted

skewbald

palomino

piebald

dun

**Bay:** Dull red, brown or yellowish coat with black mane and tail.

**Black:** All black except for the occasional white markings on the head or legs.

**Brown or Dark Brown:** A mixture of black and brown, with black mane, tail and limbs.

**Chestnut:** Ranges from a light ginger colour to a dark reddish-brown with slightly lighter or darker mane and tail.

**Cream:** Unpigmented skin. Pale chestnut hairs with cream mane and tail.

**Dun:** The body colour is light sand with black mane and tail. Dun ponies have a dark stripe along their backs and occasional zebra markings on their legs.

**Grey:** Black skin with both black and white hairs throughout, the coat varies from light to iron and dappled (mottled).

**Palomino:** The mane and tail are white, the body golden.

**Piebald:** Covered in large, irregular patches of black and white.

**Blue roan:** A black or blue coat is evenly sprinkled with white hairs. The mane and tail are black.

**Strawberry roan or Chestnut roan:** Chestnut and white hairs throughout give a 'pink' appearance.

**Skewbald:** Patches of white and any other colour except black. Both piebalds and skewbalds are known as 'Pintos' in America.

**Spotted:** There are three main types: leopard – white with any colour spots; snowflake – any colour with white spots; blanket – with a spotted rump only.

# Head and leg markings

It is not always possible to identify a horse simply by describing its colour. Instead, you may need to talk about its age, sex, height and – most helpful of all – its markings.

## Every horse unique

Nearly all domestic horses have some kind of marking (a patch of white hair, often on the legs or face). Markings can vary in shape and size and no two horses are ever exactly the same.

This means that the pattern of markings on a horse's body are his own unique record and are a great help for identification purposes.

On the face, you might find a small white 'snip' between the nostrils or an entirely white, mask-like pattern which is known as a white (or bald) face. Leg markings are equally varied and include anything from a splash of white on the heel to an irregular leg, where the white hair extends from the top of the hoof right up the leg and beyond the knee (or the hock).

Markings are not just found on the face or legs. In some breeds, like the Clydesdale, they are also common on the belly or the hindquarters.

snip

stripe

flower

star

fetlock

pastern

crown

half pastern

coronet

blaze

white face

white to stifle
in front and
above hock
behind

white knee

white muzzle

white leg

heel

fleck

white to hock

white to knee

white to
proximal fetlock

**Blaze:** A broad white band which runs the length of the face.
**Coronet:** A thin rim around the top of the hoof.
**Crown:** A semi-circle above the front of the hoof.
**Fetlock:** White hair from coronet to fetlock.
**Fleck:** A small irregular patch of white hairs.
**Flower:** This star resembles a flower shape.
**Heel:** A small patch above the rear of the hoof.
**Knee:** This reaches from hoof to knee.
**Leg:** Marking covers the whole leg. The hooves are often unpigmented (white).
**Pastern:** Extends from the hoof to the tip of the pastern.
**Snip:** A patch between the nostrils.
**Star:** Any white mark on the forehead. The exact shape, size and position should be described.
**Stripe:** A thin white line of hairs from forehead to muzzle which may join on to the star.
**White face:** A patch across the face which covers the eyes and runs towards the mouth.
**White muzzle:** This covers the nostrils, the muzzle and, usually, the upper and lower lips.
Terms such as **sock, stocking,** etc are no longer used. All markings on the limbs are described using the points of the anatomy, eg **white to fetlock, white to mid-cannon,** or **white patch on coronet – outside.**

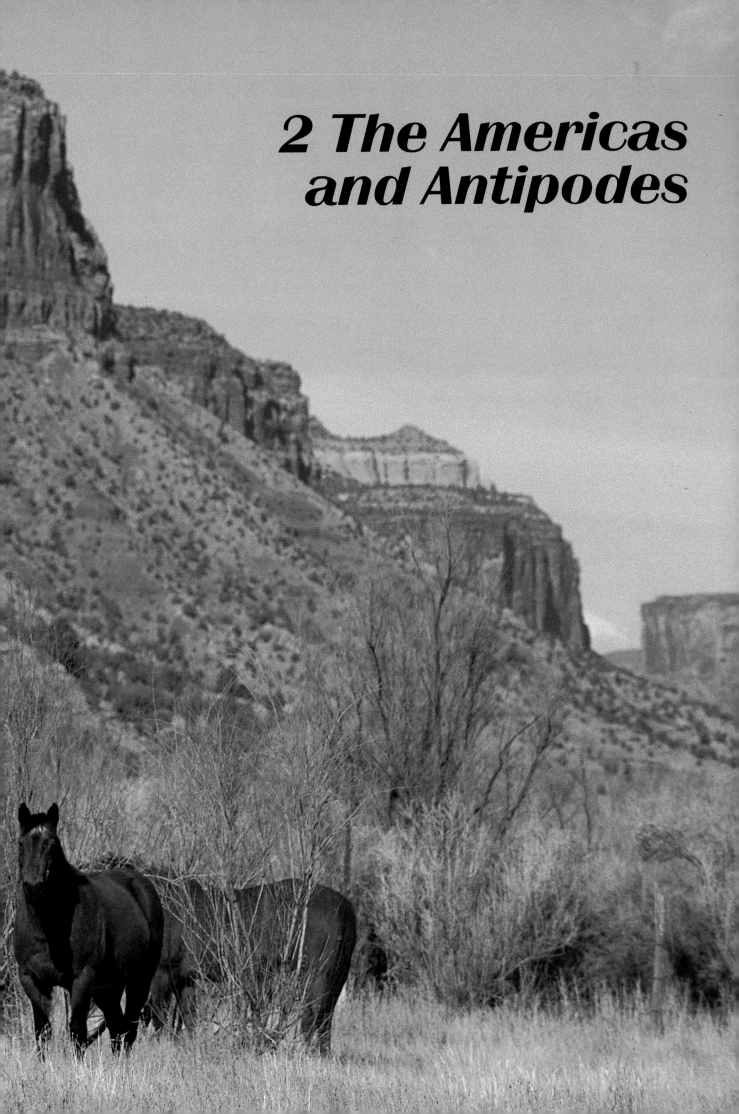

# 2 The Americas and Antipodes

# Falabella

The Falabella is a miniature horse and is one of the rarest breeds in the world. They have been bred for over a hundred years on a ranch outside Buenos Aires in Argentina.

The breed's ancestors were discovered by an Irish man called Newton (whose daughter married Señor Falabella, and gave her new name to the breed). Newton had a ranch in Argentina and nearby was a watering hole – the only one for miles around. One day a tiny horse appeared and took a drink, and Señor Newton realized it was a perfect miniature horse. He kept it and bred miniature horses from it – the offspring of this stallion was the foundation stock for the Falabella.

The development of the Falabella was by no means quick. It took many years of breeding from different horses to reach the size of today's Falabella.

Falabellas have unique features. First, they have a dominant gene for 'dwarfness' which means that even when bred with taller horses the offspring are miniature. Second, the Falabella's gestation period (pregnancy) is longer than normal; it lasts for 12–13 months instead of 11. Third, it has two less ribs and vertebrae than usual.

**Appearance:** Falabellas have all the characteristics of a horse, despite being so small.
**Height:** Under 8.5 hands.
**Colour:** Any.
**Personality:** Falabellas have steady tempers and are friendly. They are intelligent, hardy and capable of jumping. For these reasons they make ideal pets, and are sometimes even used in harness. However, they are not generally strong enough to be ridden.

Argentina

▼ **The Argentinian Falabella** only reaches a maximum height of 8.5 hands. In appearance it is like a miniature horse and can be any colour.

# Pony of the Americas

This versatile breed has existed only since the middle of the 20th century. It was developed by crossing an Appaloosa horse and a Shetland pony, to produce what could be described as a miniature Appaloosa.

In 1956 an American named Leslie Boomhower mated a Shetland stallion to an Appaloosa mare. The offspring was a colt called Black Hand, who became the foundation sire for this new breed.

A stud book has been started and only those ponies with sturdy conformation and traditional Appaloosa markings are selected for entry.

The Pony of the Americas can be seen in show rings all over North America and serves as an all-round children's pony.

**Appearance:** The body is rounded and deep through the girth, with muscular quarters and short, tough legs.
**Height:** 11.2 to 13 hands.
**Colour:** Normal Appaloosa markings appear: leopard spotted, snowflake, marble, frost and white blanket.
**Personality:** Like its ancestors, the Pony of the Americas is kind natured and easy to handle. Because of its small size, the breed is ideal for children.

▼ **The Pony of the Americas** is a newly developed breed, which is finer than the Shetland in conformation and bears Appaloosa markings.

# Brumby

Brumby is the name given to the wild horses which roam the Australian bush. There are no native breeds in Australia – just types which have been introduced by people who live there.

## Where they come from

When settlers colonized Australia in the 18th century, they brought with them their own horses for transport and communication. During the Great Gold Rush in 1851, many horses were also imported. But, when the gold ran out, the miners returned home and large numbers of horses were turned loose.

These animals flourished in the wild and multiplied. Despite not being top quality or bred to any particular plan, the offspring were sturdy and tough.

The number of Brumbies increased even more at the beginning of this century. In the Boer War of 1899–1902, and the First World War of 1914–1918, horses were gathered from all over Australia for the mounted regiments. When the wars ended, the horses left over were again set free.

## Why 'Brumbies'?

There are many tales as to the origin of the name 'Brumby'. One story goes that the horses were named after an early settler called James Brumby. He abandoned his horses in Australia in 1804.

Another legend claims that the name stems from the Aboriginal word *baroomby* which means 'wild'. Yet another idea is that the word comes from *baramba* – the name of a creek and cattle station in Queensland.

▼ **Brumbies roam wild** in the Australian countryside. They are descended from the first horses ever to tread Australia's soil.

These horses were brought from the Cape of Good Hope in South Africa, and were described as being crosses between Arabs, Persian (Iranian) horses and Barbs from North Africa.

# Criollo

The Criollo – a native of Argentina – is thought to be a relative of the Barb, Andalusian and Arab. Its ancestors were brought to South America by Spanish soldiers in the 16th century. In the fighting that followed their invasion some horses escaped into the wild, grassland areas called the 'pampas'.

The conditions here are harsh. The weather is extreme, with prairie fires, dust storms, floods and dramatic temperature changes. Only the toughest horses survived and, over 300 years of breeding naturally, they developed into the modern Criollo.

The breed is not only found in Argentina: there are variations all over South America. In Brazil it is known as the Crioulo; in Peru the Costeño; in Chile the Caballo Chilero; and in Venezuela, the Llanero.

Nowadays the Criollo is a popular ranch horse. It is most valued for cross-breeding with Thoroughbreds, combining its hardy, athletic nature with the Thoroughbred's speed to produce some of the finest polo ponies in the world.

**Appearance:** The head is broad with wide-set eyes and alert ears. The neck is muscular and the chest is wide. Its back is short and deep and the quarters are well developed. The legs are relatively short but strong and the feet are small and hard.

**Height:** 13.3 to 15.1 hands.

**Colour:** Dun with dark points and a dorsal stripe is the most usual colour. This blends in with the dry, sandy countryside of the Criollo's homeland, and is a natural camouflage.

**Personality:** Criollos are tough and intelligent. They are well known for their powers of endurance, and their quick, agile movement has made them popular with South American cowboys (gauchos) for herding cattle. They are also used for general and long-distance riding and pack work.

▼ **The nimble Criollo** is famous for its part in the breeding of polo ponies.

# Mustang

Mustangs are wild horses – their name, which has Spanish origins, means 'horses without owners'. They have existed in North America since the 16th century.

Spanish settlers brought Barb and Andalusian horses with them when they landed in America. Some of the horses broke free and inter-bred, producing large herds of Mustangs. They were used by Indians to hunt bison and cowboys later found they instinctively had excellent 'cow-sense'.

As settlers moved westward, Mustangs were bred with other types of horses brought into the USA. The Quarter Horse, for instance, is a Thoroughbred-Mustang cross.

Nowadays some are registered at studs in an attempt to preserve the original types. Many Mustangs are domesticated and used as riding and endurance horses.

**Appearance:** Conformation varies but in general Mustangs have small, sturdy bodies with tough legs.
**Height:** 13.2 to 15 hands.
**Colour:** All colours including some unusual ones: 'medicine hat' – pinto (skewbald or piebald) with dark markings on the ears; 'grulla' – black dun; 'claybank' – red dun.
**Personality:** Mustangs are hardy from living in the wild. Although they are not always even tempered they are brave.

▼ **Mustangs** are sturdy for their size and come in a wide variety of colours. Originally they were wild, and they later became a popular choice for cowboys (inset).

# Morgan

The Morgan was first bred in Massachusetts in the 1790s. The founder was a small, tough, bay colt called 'Figure' who was believed to have Welsh Cob, Thoroughbred and Arab origins.

This sturdy little horse was inherited by a man named Justin Morgan as repayment of a debt, and proved to be a great asset. Morgan put him to work ploughing and hauling timber and raced him both in harness and under saddle. He also entered the stallion for weight-pulling competitions.

Figure proved valuable for breeding with all types of mares. The offspring always inherited their sire's strength and stamina. After Justin Morgan died, breeding was taken over by the United States army at a stud in Vermont.

Some Morgans were used to form other modern-day breeds, such as the Saddlebred, the Standardbred and the Tennessee Walking Horse.

**Appearance:** The face is either straight or concave with an alert expression. The neck is crested, the shoulders are well set and the back is short. The body is compact and the quarters are rounded and muscular.

**Height:** 14.2 to 15.2 hands.

**Colour:** Bay, black, brown or chestnut.

**Personality:** Morgans are easy to handle, intelligent and enduring. They are divided into two categories: the Park horse and the Pleasure horse. The Park horse has a higher action. Both types are popular in ridden and harness classes, and are well suited to general and endurance riding.

▼ **Morgans** are very versatile and have great stamina, both characteristics they have inherited from the original sire, 'Figure'.

# Missouri Fox Trotter

The Missouri Fox Trotter was developed at the beginning of the 19th century, in the Ozark Mountains of Missouri. It is well known for its unusual, ambling gait – the 'fox trot'. The horse has a natural ability to walk in front and trot behind, which can be brought out with careful training, making it a smooth ride.

Pioneers who settled in the Ozark region brought with them Arab, Morgan and southern plantation horses. These were cross-bred to produce a riding ... for those who needed to be mobile, in par... lar doctors and sheriffs.

Later a... ns to the cross-breeding included Saddlebreds, Tennessee Walk-ing Horses and Standardbreds.

Nowadays, Fox Trotters are used for trail (long-distance) riding and some are exhibited at shows.

**Appearance:** The head is elegantly shaped with pointed ears and alert eyes. The neck is well muscled and the shoulders are sloping. The back is short and the body is compact.

**Height:** 14–16 hands.

**Colour:** Can be any colour.

**Personality:** Missouri Fox Trotters are docile and kindly natured, as well as easy to train. They are ideal riding horses, with their comfortable gait, sure-footedness and gentle character.

USA

Ozark Mountains

▼ **The comfortable gait** of the Missouri Fox Trotter makes it ideal for riding long distance.

# Peruvian Stepping Horse

The Peruvian Stepping Horse originated along similar lines to the Paso Fino. Its ancestors were Barbs and Andalusians brought to Peru by the Spanish in the 16th century.

Like the Paso Fino, the Peruvian Stepping Horse has an unusual gait known as the *Paso*. The breed is therefore sometimes known as the Peruvian Paso.

The Paso is a lateral gait with the forelegs arched and the hindquarters low as the long straight hindlegs propel the horse forward. The gait is comfortable for the rider, and the horse has the stamina to maintain speeds of up to 24kmh (15mph) over the roughest terrain for long periods of time.

Peruvian Stepping Horses are well known for being hardy enough to survive on small amounts of food. With their extraordinary gait, they are ideal for showing and are popular for long-distance riding and ranch work.

**Appearance:** The Peruvian Stepping Horse has similar conformation to the Barb, but with a slightly heavier build. However, the shoulders are sloping to allow for the high-stepping foreleg.
**Height:** 14 to 15.2 hands.
**Colour:** Usually bay or chestnut but can be most other colours.
**Personality:** The breed has remained popular because the horses are kind natured as well as enduring and tough.

▼ **The Peruvian Stepping Horse** has hardy conformation and a high-stepping, lateral gait called the *Paso*. The tack this horse is wearing is typical of Peruvian horses.

# Paso Fino

The Puerto Rican Paso Fino is a small, sturdy breed with unusual paces.

In the 1500s Andalusian, Barb and small Spanish horses, called Jennets, were taken to the Dominican Republic by Christopher Columbus. Some of these horses were taken to neighbouring Puerto Rico, where they were selectively bred to produce the Paso Fino.

From the Jennets, the Paso inherited its three lateral gaits: its fore and hindlegs move in pairs, not diagonals.

The *Paso Fino* itself is a showy, collected pace about the speed of a slow walk. The slightly faster *Paso Corto* is used for long-distance riding, and the *Paso Largo* is the fastest and most extended pace. All of these are natural to the horse.

Paso Finos excel over long distances. They feel relaxing to ride and cover ground at fast speeds. They also show off their paces in the show-ring and are used for general riding and driving.

**Appearance:** The Paso Fino has a small head. The shoulders and back are strong, with muscular quarters and tough legs.

**Height:** From 13 to 15 hands.

**Colour:** Most solid colours.

**Personality:** Paso Finos are excellent, versatile mounts. They are intelligent and kind natured.

USA    Puerto Rico

Dominican Republic

▼ **The sturdy little Paso Fino** has spectacular action. The horse moves its legs laterally — one side then the other — rather than trotting diagonally.

# Tennessee Walking Horse

The Tennessee Walking Horse, also known as the Plantation Walking Horse and the Turn Row, was developed in the 19th century. The foundation sire was a Standardbred called Black Allan. He was put to native Thoroughbred, pacer and Saddlebred mares.

Originally the breed was used to transport farmers over their tobacco and cotton plantations – the horses could travel at high speeds between rows of plants without causing any damage.

The Tennessee Walking Horse has three special paces – the flat-foot walk, the running walk and the rocking-chair canter. They are all natural to the horse and are perfected with training.

In the flat-foot walk the hind feet glide over the tracks made by the front feet and the horse nods his head in time with the movement. The running walk is a faster, more exaggerated version of the flat-foot, and the rocking-chair canter is a smooth, high-stepping pace.

Today the Tennessee Walking Horse is used for general riding and for showing in-harness and under saddle.

**Appearance:** The head is handsome and set on to a well-muscled neck. The back is short, the body is robust and the hindquarters are muscular. The croup is sloping and the tail is set high.
**Height:** 15.2 hands and over.
**Colour:** Black, bay, chestnut and occasionally grey or roan.
**Personality:** The Tennessee Walking Horse is alert and kind natured.

USA

Tennessee

▼ **The Tennessee Walking Horse's** noble appearance makes him popular for showing.

# Saddlebred

The spectacular Saddlebred, originally known as the Kentucky Saddle Horse, was bred by settlers in the southern states of America in the late 18th century. The founding sire was an English Thoroughbred called Denmark.

Saddlebreds were selectively bred to travel over great distances at high speeds. They are versatile enough to be ridden or driven in harness, and they have two special gaits – 'slow' and the faster 'rack', as well as the walk, trot and canter. Both are four-time lateral gaits, with each of the legs lifting high and landing one at a time. Although these paces come naturally to the Saddlebred, they are emphasized by training.

Today Saddlebreds are regularly seen in the show ring, where they compete in three-gaited, five-gaited and harness classes. They are also widely used for general riding.

**Appearance:** The head is attractive and set on to a slender, arched neck. The shoulders are sloping, the croup is flat and the legs are fine and strong. Both the mane and tail are full.
**Height:** 15-16 hands.
**Colour:** Usually black, bay, grey or chestnut, but occasionally roan, pinto or palomino.
**Personality:** Saddlebreds are fast and full of courage.

**▼ The Saddlebred** carries its striking head and full tail proudly. Its elegant, high-stepping paces are a pleasure to watch.

# Palomino

Palominos' golden coats and blond manes are striking. Though usually thought of as a colour not a breed, there are several breed registeries in the USA.

Palominos are relatives of the Arab and the Barb, and were prized in 15th-century Spain where the Queen supported their breeding. They were known as Golden Isabellas in her honour. When the explorer Cortez went to Mexico in the early 1500s, the Queen allowed him to take some of her favourite horses with him. He presented them to a man called Count de Palomino. This is where the modern name originated.

Later, many Palominos escaped into the wild and became part of the great Mustang herds of the United States.

Nowadays, Palominos are ridden in long-distance events, shown in many different classes – including Western and 'cutting' – and entered in jumping and driving competitions.

**Appearance:** Because Palominos are not yet a fixed breed, their build varies. Generally, they have good conformation, often similar to the Arab and the Barb.

**Height:** Palominos vary in height and can be ponies or horses.

**Colour:** Various shades of golden, from cream to darker chestnut. The mane and tail are almost white-blond and the only markings allowed are white on the face and below the knee.

**Personality:** Palominos vary in temperament according to breeding.

USA

Mexico

▼ **The Palomino** is known for its beautiful golden coat and white mane and tail. It is recognized by its colour and is not yet a true breed.

# Appaloosa

With their distinctive spotted coats, Appaloosas are often used as parade horses. They also have a kindly temperament, making them excellent all-round riding horses.

Appaloosas were first bred by the Nez Percé tribe of Washington State. Although they are now found all over the world, they are still most common in the United States.

**Appearance:** A compact horse with a short, straight back and well-developed withers. It has a deep chest, sloping shoulders, and powerful quarters and legs. The hooves are hard and often marked with vertical black and white stripes. Appaloosas have little mane or tail hair.

**Height:** 14.2 to 15.2 hands.

**Colour:** Spotted, usually on a roan background. There are six varieties of colouring: leopard (white coat with dark spots), snowflake (dark coat with white spots), marble (speckled), frost (white specks on a dark coat) and white blanket (dark coat with white quarters and loins).

**Personality:** Very sensible horses, which are exceptionally easy to handle, as well as being agile, athletic and versatile. They are good at jumping, and have considerable stamina and speed over long distances.

▼ **This Appaloosa stallion** shows typical leopard spotting. The breed is named after its place of origin: the Palouse Valley in the United States.

Palouse Valley
Canada
USA

# Pinto

The Pinto, or Paint horse, is technically only a colour, not a true breed. In America there are Pinto and Paint breed registeries, but coloured horses are found all over Europe and Asia.

Pintos were among the horses transported to South America by the Spanish explorer Cortez, in the early 16th century. Their wild descendants became popular with North American Indians because of their toughness and colouring, which provided good camouflage for war horses.

Today breeders concentrate on producing the spectacular colours, rather than standard conformation. Fortunately the Pinto gene is dominant so the colours are easy to breed on.

Pintos are so popular that some shows even have special Pinto classes. The horses are judged for their coat markings, as well as for their build and performance.

**Appearance:** Because Pintos can be seen among many breeds, their conformation varies a great deal.

**Height:** Can be any.

**Colour:** Pintos come in two types of colouring: white with brown or bay patches and black with white patches. In Britain the brown and white colouring is called skewbald and black and white patches are known as piebald.

The coat patterns come in two main types, 'Overo' describes a coat with white patches starting from the belly. 'Tobiano' colouring has white patches beginning on the back. They have more defined patches of colour which are usually solid. Tobianos are often larger than Overos.

**Personality:** Pintos vary in temperament, depending on their breeding. They are often seen in the show ring because they are so striking. They are also used as cow ponies and for many different kinds of leisure riding.

▼ **This eyecatching Pinto** has a Tobiano coat pattern. The combination of solid brown and white patches is known as skewbald in the British Isles.

# Canadian Cutting Horse

The Cutting horse is a principal breed of Canada. In the days of cattle ranching on horseback, these horses were in great demand. Nowadays they are popular for Cutting and Western riding competitions and for pleasure riding.

They are named after the technique of 'cutting'. This means singling out an animal and isolating it from the rest of the herd. The horse needs to be fast and agile – to be able to twist and turn at sharp angles, and at top speed – preventing the selected steer from returning to its herd.

Most Cutting horses are derived from American Quarter Horses, to which they are very similar.

**Appearance:** The Cutting horse has excellent conformation for a ranch horse. Its shoulders are muscular and strong, with a short back and well-developed hindquarters. These qualities enable it to move at great speed as it 'cuts' in and out of the herd.

**Height:** 15.2 to 16.1 hands.

**Colour:** Usually black, brown or bay, but also most other solid colours (not skewbald or piebald).

**Personality:** Cutting horses are intelligent and begin training from a young age. They are taught to respond to the slightest aids and so appear to work without their riders having to make any demands of them.

▼ **The intelligent,** muscular Canadian Cutting horse is closely related to the Quarter Horse from the United States of America.

# Waler

The Australian Waler was first bred in New South Wales, from where it takes its name. This hard-working horse has played a key role in the development of Australia as a nation.

When Europeans first started to colonize Australia in the late 18th century, they took with them Basuto ponies from South Africa. Soon after, Arabs, Barbs and Thoroughbreds were imported, too. These were the foundation stock of the Waler, which appeared within 40 years of settlement.

The Waler is agile and courageous and has great powers of endurance. First used for cattle and sheep work, it could carry a farmer all day round the giant ranches of Australia.

Later, it became a popular cavalry horse, both with the Australian army and with troops in India and South Africa. 16,000 Walers served in the Boer War and 121,000 in the First World War.

Today, these good-natured beasts still work on the sheep stations of Australia. They are also in demand as police and cavalry mounts, and love to play to the crowd at rodeo tournaments.

**Appearance:** The Waler is a robust version of its ancestor the Thoroughbred, with a strong back and quarters and a light forehand. It is heavy boned with good limbs.
**Height:** 14.2-16 hands.
**Colour:** Any whole colour.
**Personality:** The Waler is even-tempered and has much stamina. It is speedy, agile and brave, and is ideally suited to police and ranch work.

Australia

New South Wales

▼ **Capable of working at a gallop** over long distances, the Waler is the number one choice of Australian ranchers.

# Quarter Horse

The versatile Quarter Horse was first bred in the 17th century by English settlers in Virginia and North and South Carolina. The horses are named after the quarter-mile sprints they ran through villages or over makeshift tracks.

Quarter Horses were developed by crossing Thoroughbreds with native mares – relatives of the horses brought to America by Spanish explorers.

The founding sire was an English Thoroughbred, named Janus, who went to America in the 17th century. Although he was successful over distances of four miles, his offspring ran at top speeds over the shorter course.

Quarter Horses serve well as cow ponies, too. As well as being fast, they are agile, twisting and turning sharply as they 'cut' (single out) animals from their herds. Nowadays, the breed is also popular for showing, competing in rodeos and general leisure riding.

**Appearance:** The head is broad between the eyes, with small ears. The chest is wide and the body is very compact, around a heavy frame. The back, loins and hindquarters are solid muscle, giving the Quarter Horse take-off power, and the strength to propel itself forward when racing. The muscular hindquarters also provide the strength to turn at sharp angles when cutting.

**Height:** 15.1 to 16.1 hands.

**Colour:** Usually chestnut, but they can be any solid colour.

**Personality:** Quarter Horses are very popular because they combine athleticism with calm natures.

▼ **The Quarter Horse** has especially strong hindquarters. These give him the power to sprint over quarter-mile courses at high speed and turn sharply when cutting.

# Standardbred

The Standardbred is the world's fastest harness racehorse, both as a trotter and pacer. Not suprisingly, it has Thoroughbred ancestors – the founding sire of the Standardbred was a Thoroughbred called Hambletonian, foaled in 1849. Most modern Standardbreds trace back to one of his sons. Other original breeding stock included American Morgans, and Hackneys from England.

In 1879 the National Association of Trotting Horse Breeders laid down a set of rules for Standardbreds being admitted into the American Trotter Register. The horses had to be able to cover 1.6km (1 mile) in a time limit of two and a half minutes to qualify for entry.

Nowadays, Standardbreds are such excellent quality that they are exported all over the world to upgrade other harness racehorses.

**Appearance:** Similar to the Thoroughbred although the Standardbred is shorter and slightly more thick-set. The body is deep through the girth, the hindquarters have plenty of muscle and the legs are strong and sturdy.
**Height:** An average of 15.2 hands.
**Colour:** Any solid colour.
**Personality:** Standardbreds are powerful and courageous.

▼ **The Standardbred** is built for racing, with sturdy legs and a strong body. It is the fastest harness racehorse in the world and is bred mainly in Kentucky.

# Shetland

Shetland ponies are thought to have inhabited the islands just north of Scotland for thousands of years.

Shetlands are well adapted to this harsh environment. They have two-layered coats for warmth and water-proofing in winter. They can survive on small quantities of food, and their size means they can shelter from the weather behind rocks when there are no trees. Although they are so small, they are very strong in relation to their size.

Shetlands were at one time the only means of transport on the islands. They carried heavy packs as well as people.

Because the islands are so isolated, the ponies remained pure-bred for centuries. This changed, however, when the coal-mining industry began to boom in northern England and Wales. Shetlands were ideal for work in the mines – they were small enough to fit in the mine shafts and tough enough to pull heavy coal wagons. Many were taken from the islands and cross-bred to produce pit ponies. To preserve the pure form of the breed, studs were set up on the Shetland islands of Bressay and Noss.

Nowadays Shetlands are popular riding ponies, particularly with children. They are also good at driving.

**Appearance:** The head is small, with neat ears and large eyes. The neck is strong, the back is relatively short and the body is deep through the girth. The short legs are very sturdy and the hooves are tough. The mane and tail are full, with the tail set high.

**Height:** Shetlands are measured in centimetres/inches in Britain, rather than in hands, as they are in the United States. As 3 year-olds they can be up to 102cm (40in), and at 4 years and over they can be up to 107cm (42in).

**Colour:** Any colouring except spotted.

**Personality:** Shetlands are generally intelligent and gentle.

Shetland Islands
Atlantic Ocean
Scotland

▼ **This handsome Shetland stallion** is typically small and sturdy. His mane and tail are full and his summer coat is silky.

# Welsh Mountain Pony

Welsh Mountain Ponies have grazed the hills and moors of Wales for over a thousand years. When Julius Caesar came to Britain with the Romans, he thought they were the most beautiful ponies in Britain and started a stud farm.

Ever since then, the Welsh Mountain Pony has been much used for cross-breeding. It was the foundation stock for the Polo Pony, the Riding Pony, the Hack, and the Hunter. The mares were probably used in the early development of the Thoroughbred.

The Welsh Mountain Pony has been exported to other countries more than any other British pony and foreign breeders have paid high prices for it.

In spite of their small size, they are strong and can carry an adult with ease. They were often used as pit ponies in 19th century coal-mines.

Today, herds of wild ponies still graze the mountains in Wales. When tame, they are excellent jumpers and show ponies. The breed is in great demand all over the world as a riding pony for children and beginners.

**Appearance:** Welsh Mountain Ponies are like miniature Arabs. Their elegant heads are small with neat, pointed ears and bold, intelligent eyes. From the side, the face is dished, suggesting Arab blood. The neck is long and set on sloped-back shoulders. The withers are well defined and the legs are set square. Their tails are raised high.

**Height:** Up to 12.2 hands.

**Colour:** Any solid colour.

**Personality:** Welsh Mountain Ponies are intelligent, courageous and tough from their hard lives in the hills.

England

Wales

▼ **Welsh Mountain Ponies** are brave and good natured. This sturdy breed makes an excellent child's riding pony.

# Welsh Pony

The Welsh Pony is a larger, more modern version of the Welsh Mountain Pony. Both are descended from the spirited horses that roamed free in the hills of Wales in Roman times.

The Welsh Pony was originally bred by hill farmers who used them for transport and shepherding work in the mountain pastures. Welsh Mountain Ponies, Welsh Cobs, small Thoroughbreds and Arabs were the foundation stock of the breed. Though their breeding encouraged riding qualities, Welsh Ponies kept the characteristics of hardiness and intelligence that they had inherited from their Welsh Mountain ancestors.

In the 19th century, they were widely used as pit ponies in Wales. They took over from women and young boys hauling large tubs from the coal-face to the mine-shafts. In 1911, a law controlled their working hours and ensured that these unflagging ponies experienced less hardship than many of the other horses working in industry.

The Welsh Pony has been used as foundation stock for many types and breeds including the Hackney, the Hack, the Polo Pony, and the Riding Pony.

Today, the Welsh Pony is one of the most common riding breeds in the USA.

**Appearance:** The Welsh Pony is similar to the Welsh Mountain, but is larger and more of a riding type. It has a neat, intelligent head with a bold eye.
**Height:** Under 13.2 hands.
**Colour:** Any colour except piebald or skewbald.
**Personality:** Welsh Ponies' gentleness, courage, intelligence and toughness make them ideal riding ponies.

▼ **The Welsh Pony** is one of the most attractive of British native breeds. Exported all over the world, it has been used as the foundation stock for many types and breeds.

# *Exmoor*

Exmoor is an area of moorland which covers the far west of Somerset and part of north Devon. The herds of ponies that live wild on the moor are named after their home. They are the oldest and purest of the British breeds.

Fossils thought to be of the Exmoor's ancestors have been found in Alaska dating back to the Ice Age. It is believed that these ponies travelled to Europe when the continents were joined by land. Those that settled in south-west England remained there and developed into today's Exmoor.

A breed similar to the Exmoor was established by the time the Romans invaded England. Indeed, their armies met fierce resistance from tribes who used Exmoor-types for pulling chariots.

Nowadays Exmoors roam wild on the moors in herds but every autumn they are rounded up and the best examples are entered in the breed stud book. They are branded with an individual number on the left hindquarter, a herd number and the Exmoor Society's star on the near shoulder. They are then released into the wild again.

**Appearance:** Exmoors have short ears and a wide forehead. The eyes are prominent and have a heavy top lid giving them a hooded appearance (this is known as 'toad eyes'). The neck is short and thick, the chest is deep and the back is broad. Exmoors have short, strong legs. Their coats are thick and waterproof in winter and short and shiny in summer. The tail is thick and has a fan-shaped growth at the top.

**Height:** Mares are up to 12.2 hands; stallions and geldings up to 12.3.

**Colour:** Bay, brown or mouse-dun with black points. The Exmoor has a mealy mouth (speckled fawn colour). This colouring also appears on the belly and between the thighs.

**Personality:** Exmoors are intelligent, hardy and enduring. They have been used as pack animals and for sheep herding, and nowadays they are popular for trekking, showing and driving. If they are treated patiently and kindly, Exmoors make ideal children's ponies, and are used as mounts for the disabled. They are also strong enough to carry adults.

Exmoor

▲ ▼ **Exmoor ponies,** the oldest of the native British breeds, roam wild on the moor in south-west England after which they are named. These plucky but kind ponies are easily identified by their light-coloured, mealy noses.

# Dartmoor

Dartmoor, in Devon (England), is both the home and the name of a native breed of sure-footed ponies that have roamed the blustery moors for hundreds of years.

In 1899 the Polo Pony Society – later to become the National Pony Society – introduced set standards for the breeding of Dartmoors. But the boom of the mining industry, in the early 20th century, led to some Shetland ponies being introduced on Dartmoor. The crosses with native ponies resulted in a tough but smaller pony, suitable for working below ground in the mines.

Later, in 1924, the Dartmoor Pony Society formed, and concentrated on breeding Dartmoors 'true to type'.

**Appearance:** The Dartmoor has a small, attractive head, with bright eyes and alert ears. The neck is strong and the back is muscular. The quarters, legs and feet are all well formed, giving the Dartmoor a good overall conformation. The mane and tail are full, with the tail high-set.

**Height:** Not exceeding 12.2 hands.

**Colour:** Bay, brown, black, occasionally grey, roan or chestnut. Skewbald and piebald are not accepted but small white markings are allowed for showing.

**Personality:** The Dartmoor has a kind and sensible temperament which, together with its conformation, makes it an ideal first-time pony and a mount for children. Dartmoors can be used for jumping, hunting and driving and are also strong enough to carry adults.

Dartmoor  Devon

▼ **Dartmoor ponies** have lived on the moors in Devon for hundreds of years. When domesticated they make ideal mounts, as they are good natured and adaptable.

# New Forest

The New Forest, in Hampshire, is the home – and the name – of one of the biggest Mountain and Moorland breeds.

Ponies have lived in the New Forest since the 11th century. They are believed to be the ancestors of the sturdy little ponies which live there today.

The pasture in the Forest is sometimes sparse, providing only heather and low-quality grass. New Forest ponies have learned to adapt to these poor resources, becoming hardy and sure-footed in their search for food.

Over the years, New Forest ponies cross-bred with other native horses which roamed the countryside. At some stages, breeds were deliberately introduced to upgrade existing stock. In 1852, for example, Queen Victoria allowed her Arab stallion, Zora, to be set free among the herds for eight years.

**Appearance:** New Forest ponies have attractive, 'pony-like' heads. Their shoulders are sloping and their bodies are deep but narrow, with short backs. The quarters are strong and the legs and feet are tough.

**Height:** New Forests fall into two categories: A – up to 13.2 hands; B – 13.2-14.2 hands.

**Colour:** Any colour except piebald and skewbald.

**Personality:** New Forest ponies are intelligent and docile. They make excellent family mounts, because they are both strong enough to carry adults and narrow enough for children to ride. Because the Forest is popular with tourists and has roads going through it, the ponies are used to people and are not 'traffic shy'. Their popularity has now spread all over the world.

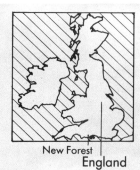

New Forest | England

▼ **Ponies** in the New Forest survive on poor rations. Those that live there today are hardy as a result.

# Connemara

The Connemara is an attractive pony, named after the area of Connaught, in the south west of the Republic of Ireland. Its home is the bleak, rocky moorlands.

Although its history is unclear, several tales explain its origins. One legend has it that the Connemara's ancestors were the surviving horses of the Spanish Armada fleet, which was shipwrecked off the western coast of Ireland in 1588.

Another theory is that merchants from Galway, who traded with the Spaniards, bought Spanish horses and crossed them with native Irish stock. It has also been suggested that Connemaras are related to the horses used by the Celtic people who settled in the British Isles as long ago as the 4th century.

Connemaras are bred all over Europe, Australia and America, and compete in most equestrian activities: dressage, show jumping, cross country, long-distance riding, hunting and driving.

**Appearance:** The head is small with dark eyes and small ears. It is set on an arched neck and sloping shoulders. The body is compact and deep through the girth, the legs are short and the hindquarters are strong, with the tail high-set.

**Height:** 13 to 14.2 hands.

**Colour:** Originally Connemaras were dun with black points and a stripe down the middle of the back. Nowadays they are most often grey, also dun, brown, bay, black, roan or chestnut.

**Personality:** The wild environment of the Connemara's home only provides rough grass for them to live on. They have had to become hardy to survive.

They are intelligent, gentle and strong, making them ideal for both adults and children to ride.

▼ **The hardy Connemara** is a native of the bleak moors in County Galway, which is part of the Connaught province in Ireland.

Originally Connemaras were dun with black points (inset).

# Dales

These versatile ponies come from the eastern hills of the Pennine range.

Many breeds – including the extinct Scotch Galloway, the Wilson pony (now the Hackney pony) and the Norfolk and Yorkshire Roadsters (trotters) – played a part in the development of the Dales we know today.

Until the middle of the 19th century, Dales were bred as pack animals. Despite being small they can carry up to 126kg (about 20 stone, or 280 pounds) and pull up to a ton.

In both World Wars Dales were used by artillery regiments. After the Second World War the breed was in danger of extinction, but was saved by the efforts of breeders and the Dales Pony Society.

**Appearance:** The head is neat and pony-like. The eyes are wide-set and the ears are inwardly curving. Its strong neck is set on to sloping shoulders and a broad chest. The quarters are powerful, the legs are of good quality with plenty of feather; the feet are hard and well-shaped. The mane and tail are long.
**Height:** Up to 14.2 hands.
**Colour:** Black, sometimes brown, grey and bay and occasionally roan.
**Personality:** Dales ponies are intelligent and sensible. They are fast, stylish trotters and are good at jumping. Nowadays they are popular for trekking, harness work, jumping and general riding. Dales carry both adults and children, but are not recommended for novices as they are very strong.

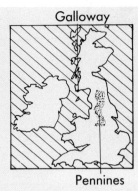

Galloway

Pennines

▼ **Dales ponies** have been given the name which describes their homeland: the low dales set between the Pennine hills.

# Fell

The Fell's home is the western Pennine hills and the mountains of Cumbria in northern England. Its ancestors were the Scotch Galloway pony and the Dutch Friesian.

Like their neighbours the Dales, Fell ponies were used for transporting lead from the mines to the Tyneside docks in the 19th century. The ponies carried lead-filled panniers (packs either side of the saddle) and were driven in groups of up to twenty, by one mounted man. Fells were also popular for shepherding, farmwork, pulling carts, riding and sports such as trotting races.

The work of the Fell Pony Society has made the Fell one of the purest of Britain's Mountain and Moorland breeds. Fells are increasing in number because they make good all-round family ponies.

**Appearance:** The Fell has a small head with a broad forehead and neat ears. The shoulders are long and sloping; the back and hindquarters are strong. Although the legs are short they are tough and the hooves are round and open. There is plenty of feather and the mane and tail are long and thick.

**Height:** Up to 14 hands.

**Colour:** Most often black, sometimes bay, brown or grey. Small white markings are allowed.

**Personality:** Fells are energetic and hardy. Because their homeland is very hilly they are naturally sure footed.

Nowadays they are popular for taking tourists trekking, for riding and for driving. Some are also used for hunting. Fells are exported all over the world to improve other native breeds.

Cumbria Tyneside

Pennines

▼ **The Fell** has been given the name that describes its homeland — the hills of the Pennine range.

# Highland

The Highland pony is the largest and strongest of the British Mountain and Moorland breeds. Its homeland is the highlands of Scotland and the islands off the west coast.

Although the exact origins of the Highland are not clear, it has existed in Scotland for centuries. Outside blood has been added, particularly Arab.

There are two types of Highland: the Garron from the mainland, and the Western Isles pony, which is smaller and more nimble. Nowadays cross-breeding is merging the two types.

Highlands are very versatile and over the years they have had to adapt to all sorts of work, including transport and packwork; dragging felled trees for the forestry industry; pulling farm carts and shepherding.

These sturdy, sure-footed ponies were also ridden for sports in the countryside, such as hunting.

**Appearance:** Highlands have broad faces with bright eyes and short ears. The neck is arched and strong, the chest deep and compact. The back is short and the quarters are powerful. The legs are well feathered and the mane and tail hair is silky and full.

**Height:** 13-14.2 hands.

**Colour:** All shades of dun, brown, black and grey, mostly with dark points. There is usually a dorsal stripe and sometimes zebra markings on the legs.

**Personality:** Highland ponies are strong and adaptable, intelligent and docile. They are still used as work horses in some parts of Scotland, but are more often ridden for pleasure, particularly by tourists on trekking holidays and also by disabled people.

Highlands are valuable as breeding stock for hunters and eventers and pure-breds have also been successful in driving competitions.

▼ **The versatile Highland** has the strength to cope with most types of work as well as being docile enough to carry disabled riders.

# Riding Pony

As showing classes and riding became more popular in Britain during the 20th century, there was a greater demand for elegant, good-quality ponies. This led to selective breeding and the development of the modern Riding Pony.

Native British Mountain and Moorland ponies were chosen – most frequently they were Welsh, Dartmoor or Exmoor – and were crossed with Thoroughbreds and Arabs.

The resulting breed is strong and sure-footed like its native ancestors, and good looking like its hot-blooded relatives. Riding Ponies fall into two categories: elegant, high-quality animals and slightly more sturdy hunter types.

British Riding Ponies are most commonly seen in the show ring, where they are judged on both their conformation and performance. The hunters have special classes – they are either jumped in Working Hunter Pony classes or shown in Ridden Show Hunter classes. They all make excellent hacks and leisure ponies.

Riding ponies are not just found in Britain, however. There are also special showing classes in Australia.

**Appearance:** Riding Ponies have 'pony-like' heads, with bright eyes and small ears. Their bodies are compact and strong as well as elegant.
**Height:** Up to 15 hands.
**Colour:** Any solid colour.
**Personality:** Riding ponies have kind, steady natures, just like most Mountain and Moorland breeds. They are also graceful – an inheritance from their hot-blooded breeding.

▼**Catherston Night Safe** is a handsome example of a British Riding Pony. The breed became official in 1983, when a stud book opened.

# Hackney Horse and Pony

The Hackney is a British breed familiar to many for its extraordinary high-stepping action. It was developed in the 18th century from trotting horses called Norfolk and Yorkshire Roadsters.

One of the most famous sires was called Shales, the grandson of the Thoroughbred Flying Childers – who was a descendant of the Darley Arabian (a founder of the Thoroughbred).

The invention of the railways in the 19th century put many Roadsters out of work. But the Hackney Horse Society came to the rescue, and Hackneys – as they became known – are now popular as pleasure horses.

The Hackney Pony shares much the same history as the Hackney Horse. The pony was also based on Norfolk Roadster stock. To begin with, the ponies were named after Christopher Wilson – one of the first breeders – but became known as Hackney Ponies. They are smaller versions of the horse, but retain the look and characteristics of a pony.

**Appearance:** The Hackney has a slightly convex (outwardly curving) head with small ears, large eyes and a small muzzle. The neck is long and well formed, and the body is compact. The tail is set and carried high, and the coat is silky.

**Height:** Ponies up to 14 hands; horses over 14 hands.

**Colour:** Bay, dark brown, black and chestnut.

**Personality:** Hackneys are high-spirited animals, with a spectacular trotting action. The forelegs are picked up high and the feet are thrust forward, making a rounded movement. Hackney ponies have a slightly more pronounced action than the horses, with the knees raised as high as possible and the hocks reaching right under the body, sometimes almost touching it.

Because of their grace and presence, Hackneys are popular in the show ring as harness and carriage horses for modern-day, competitive events.

Yorkshire

Norfolk

▼ **This Hackney Pony** displays the high-stepping action characteristic of the breed.

# Spotted Pony

Spotted ponies have existed in Britain since the Middle Ages, though no one knows where they came from.

For centuries these cobby ponies were used for everyday work. They were also ridden in combat, both in war and in jousting tournaments. As horses became more popular in Britain during the 15th century many ponies disappeared. The Spotted pony, however, remained in favour, especially in Wales and south-west England. By the mid-19th century it was much in evidence as a riding and driving pony.

In 1946 the British Spotted Horse and Pony Society was formed to register top-class animals and make their breeding official. In 1976 the society was split into two and the British Pony Society was set up for animals up to 14.2 hands high.

Today Spotted ponies are bred for driving, showing, eventing, jumping, long-distance riding competitions and Pony Club events.

**Appearance:** Although they vary in type, Spotted ponies generally have a good, sturdy conformation, with strong limbs.
**Height:** Up to 14.2 hands.
**Colour:** Leopard spotted, blanket and snowflake markings.
**Personality:** Spotted ponies are usually steady natured and hardy.

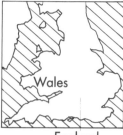

Wales

England

▼ **Spotted ponies** can often be seen in driving competitions. This eye-catching team all have leopard spotted coat markings.

# Welsh Cob

The bold, muscular Welsh Cob has been bred in Wales for many centuries. Its ancestors were Andalusians living on the Welsh borders in the 11th century. These were crossed with native Welsh Mountain Ponies to produce the Cob.

The Cob was very popular on hilly Welsh farms. It was strong enough to pull the farmer's family to church on Sunday and co-operative enough to be used for hunting. Its great strength also made it popular with the army, who would pay high prices for good stallions because of their ability to haul huge guns over rough land.

The Welsh Cob has a fast trotting style and its high-stepping action has influenced many trotting breeds of the world. It is used today for riding and harness work, especially team driving events. Few breeds do better at international shows. In-hand classes for Welsh Cobs are a popular attraction in Wales.

**Appearance:** The Welsh Cob's head is alert and pony like, with bold eyes set well apart. The neck is long and well crested, the shoulders are strong and the body is deep girthed. The short, powerful legs have tufts of silky hair at the heels.
**Height:** 14-15.2 hands.
**Colour:** Any colour except piebald or skewbald.
**Personality:** The Welsh Cob is fiery and courageous with enormous powers of endurance. It is one of the world's best riding and driving animals and is certainly one of the most versatile.

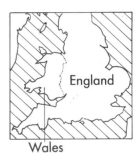

▼ **The Welsh Cob** is still used for farmwork in some parts of Wales, but it is most famous today as a harness animal in team driving events.

# Anglo-Arab

The Anglo-Arab is a mix of two of the world's finest breeds, the Arab and the English Thoroughbred. The aim is to combine the best qualities of both, to produce an excellent riding horse.

**Appearance:** Like the classical Arab it has an elegant head, with a broad forehead and bold, alert eyes. The profile is straighter than that of the Arab, tapering off to well-opened nostrils. The neck is long and set on to strong, sloping shoulders, and the back is muscular. The tail is set high and carried proudly. With its long legs and well-shaped feet, the Anglo-Arab moves lightly and gracefully.

**Height:** 15.3 to 16.3 hands.

**Colour:** Bay, brown and chestnut.

**Personality:** A willing and intelligent horse, which possesses soundness, stamina and speed. The Anglo-Arab has become highly successful in a wide range of competitive sports such as showing, show jumping, dressage and three-day eventing.

▼ **This Anglo-Arab** shows the quality and elegance that is the result of crossing two of the world's finest breeds — the Arab and the Thoroughbred.

# Thoroughbred

The Thoroughbred is the fastest of all horses. The development of this world-famous breed began in England in the late 17th and early 18th centuries.

Arab, Barb and Turkish horses were imported to improve the existing racing stock. Among these imports were the three founding sires of the present day Thoroughbred – Byerley Turk, Darley Arabian and Godolphin Barb.

In 1690 Byerley Turk was put to stud, covering a variety of native and imported mares. In 1704 Darley Arabian began siring foals and later, during the 1730s, Godolphin Barb was put to mares of the developing Thoroughbred. All modern-day Thoroughbreds can be traced back to one of these three horses.

In 1791 a stud book was established and today the British National Thoroughbred Stud is in Newmarket.

Thoroughbreds fall into four categories. Classic/middle distance racers and sprinters mature early. They are compact and run at high speeds. Stayers are slightly more wiry. They have greater stamina, so they can run longer races than the others, but are not as fast. Steeplechasers are not fast enough for flat racing, but have stamina and jumping ability.

Thoroughbreds are exported all over the world and stud books have been opened in many countries.

**Appearance:** Conformation is varied, but generally the head looks elegant and intelligent. The neck is arched and the withers are pronounced. The sloping shoulders lead into a relatively short back. The body is deep and the quarters have great strength.
**Height:** On average 15.3 to 16.1 hands.
**Colour:** Most whole colours.
**Personality:** The Thoroughbred is courageous but highly strung.

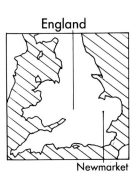

▼ **The Thoroughbred** is the fastest horse on earth. It was developed in England, and is now found all over the world.

# Irish Draught

The light, versatile Irish Draught has existed since the end of the 18th century. Its ancestors are thought to have been horses bred in Ireland's Connemara region.

The Irish Draught became popular when there was a demand for horses strong enough to carry out pack work and farming, and yet light enough to be ridden to hounds and pull the family trap at a steady trot. The Irish Draught was also popular with the army because it had strength and speed, but was economical to feed.

Today Irish Draught brood (breeding) mares and English Thoroughbred stallions are crossed to produce some of the finest Irish Hunters. They are also widely used as breeding stock for general riding horses and for some of the world's top class competition horses, particularly in show jumping.

**Appearance:** The head and neck are carried gracefully, the eyes are well set and the ears are long. The back is strong and the body is deep through the girth. There is strength in the loins and the quarters, which are sloping.

**Height:** Stallions are 16 hands and over and mares from 15.2 hands.

**Colour:** Any whole colour. White markings are allowed on the face and legs – below the hock and the knee.

**Personality:** Irish Draught horses are cold-blooded in character; they are kind and intelligent, with gentle natures. Nowadays, although they are no longer required as workers, they are still important as breeding stock and many are shown, hunted and jumped. Some Irish Draughts take part in dressage and hunter trials. Irish Draught horse societies in Ireland and England have their own, annual breed shows.

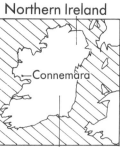

Northern Ireland

Connemara

Republic of Ireland

▼ **The Irish Draught** is a versatile breed, capable of most types of work. Nowadays it is valuable as breeding stock.

# Irish Hunter

A Hunter is a horse bred originally for hunting. It can be any size, but must be able to carry a rider, at high speeds, across all types of country. Hunters, therefore, must be courageous and athletic. Many inherit their sure-footedness and courage from native breeds.

Irish Hunters are some of the best in the world. The Irish countryside is well suited to breeding and rearing them. The miles of natural hedges and banks are perfect for training youngsters to hunt, and make most Irish horses fearless jumpers at an early age.

Irish Hunters are a type rather than a breed and were first developed by crossing Irish Draught mares with Thoroughbreds. Connemara blood has also been used in the development of the Irish Hunter.

Both British and Irish Hunters are categorized according to the weight they can carry; there are three classes.

**Lightweight:** These horses carry up to 79kg (12½ stone).
**Middleweight:** These horses carry 79–89kg (12½–14 stone).
**Heavyweight:** These horses carry over 89kg (14 stone).

There are also Ladies' Hunters. These must be able to carry a lady side-saddle in the field.

Nowadays most Irish competition horses are from the middleweight Hunter bracket.

**Appearance:** Irish Hunters are strong and agile. Most have intelligent heads and sturdy, workman-like bodies.
**Height:** From 14.2 to 17.2 hands.
**Colour:** Any colour.
**Personality:** Irish Hunters have plenty of courage and stamina, thanks to their breeding and early training, and are intelligent and versatile.

Note: A stone is a British unit of measure that equals 14 pounds.

▼ **Irish Hunters** have often become showjumpers and Irish Hunter mares have been crossed with Thoroughbreds to produce lighter versions like this one.

# Cleveland Bay

The Cleveland Bay was first bred in the county of Cleveland, in north-east England, as long ago as the 17th century. It is one of the country's oldest breeds.

Before the days of mechanical transport it was a coach horse – used in ceremonies as well as for everyday work. It was also valued by farmers for light agricultural tasks.

The breed was once known as the Chapman horse, named after 'chapmen' (travelling business men) who used Clevelands as pack horses.

Crosses with Thoroughbreds in the 19th century resulted in the development of the Yorkshire Coach horse – a lighter variation of the Cleveland – which was bred to pull more fashionable forms of transport in London. Today Clevelands are still crossed with Thoroughbreds to produce hunters, jumpers and fast carriage horses.

**Appearance:** The Cleveland Bay has a large head, with a convex (outwardly curving) face, and big expressive eyes. The neck is slender, the body is wide and deep and the hindquarters and legs are muscular. The tail is high-set.

**Height:** 16 to 16.2 hands.

**Colour:** Bay with black points – legs, mane and tail. There are sometimes grey hairs in the mane and tail but the only marking acceptable for showing is a small white star on the face.

**Personality:** Despite being large and strong, Cleveland Bays are docile and easy to school. They are intelligent and sensible, with a good deal of stamina, and live to a ripe old age.

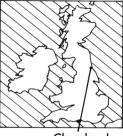

Cleveland

▲ ▼ **Cleveland Bays**, from north-east England, are one of the country's most popular carriage-horse breeds. Here, the Duke of Edinburgh puts his team through their paces in a four-in-hand competition.

# Clydesdale

These 'gentle giants' originated in the Clyde valley, in the county of Lanarkshire, Scotland.

In the middle of the 18th century, local farmers bred them to carry out draught work. The native mares were crossed with Flemish stallions, to create the Clydesdale we know today.

At the beginning of the Industrial Revolution in Great Britain, when the coal industry boomed, the Clydesdale's strength was employed for hauling coal. As road surfaces improved and pack animals were replaced with horse-drawn transport, larger, stronger horses were needed: the Clydesdale was ideal.

Today they are popular for showing and competing in ploughing matches. They have also been successfully cross-bred with Thoroughbreds to produce heavyweight riding horses and hunters.

**Appearance:** The Clydesdale has a flat face, with a wide muzzle and flared nostrils. The eyes are alert and the ears are long. Its arched neck is set into sloping shoulders, the withers are high and the back is short and strong. The quarters and gaskins (second thighs) are muscular. The Clydesdale has round, wide feet. Its tail is high-set, and there is long, silky feather on the legs.

**Height:** Stallions are 17.1 to 18 hands: mares are 16.3 to 17.2 hands.

**Colour:** Brown, bay and black are the most popular colours. There is plenty of white on the legs, over the knees and hocks, on the face and sometimes the body.

**Personality:** Clydesdales are kindly tempered and easy to train. With the combination of their excellent character and power, they are ideal work horses.

Clyde River
Lanarkshire

▲ **The Clydesdale** comes from the county of Lanarkshire in Scotland.

▼ **This handsome pair of Clydesdales** is competing in a ploughing match in the south of England.

The competitors are judged on how straight they plough the furrow (trench), on the turn-out and action of the horses and also on the appearance of the tack.

# Suffolk Punch

The Suffolk Punch, also known as the Suffolk Horse, is a strong, handsome cold-blood from the county of Suffolk in south-east England.

There are claims that this agile draught horse existed as early as the 16th century, but today's Suffolks can all be traced back to one stallion foaled in 1760. Although it is one of the purest breeds of cold-blood, the Suffolk Punch has been influenced by horses such as the Norfolk Trotter, the Thoroughbred and cobs.

Suffolks are ideal workers – they can begin work from the age of two and continue until they are as old as twenty. They are economical to keep and have great strength.

Nowadays, Suffolks are a common sight at the showground, appearing in-hand or in harness classes. In a few areas of England they are still put to work by farmers. Some are bred with Arabs and Thoroughbreds to produce heavyweight riding horses.

**Appearance:** The head is big, with a wide forehead. The neck is thick, particularly at the shoulders, which are muscular. The body is deep through the girth, the quarters are well muscled and the legs are strong but short in proportion to the body. Unlike most other cold-bloods, the Suffolk has little or no feather on the legs.

**Height:** About 16 hands.

**Colour:** All shades of chestnut. White markings on the face are acceptable.

**Personality:** Suffolks are good tempered and hard working.

Suffolk

England

▼ **Suffolk Punches** still work the land in some parts of England. The breed also makes a spectacular entrant in the show ring (inset).

# Shire

The magnificent Shire is the biggest of the English heavy horse breeds and comes from the shire counties of the Midlands – Leicestershire, Warwickshire, Northamptonshire and Lincolnshire.

The breed's origins are uncertain, but it is believed the Shire is related to the big horses that provided transport and pulling power as far back as the late 16th century.

Shires were once a common sight in the English countryside. They were valuable because they worked from as young as three years old and were capable of pulling loads of up to five times their own body-weight.

In recent years modern machinery has replaced most work horses but Shires continue to be popular. Although they are still used for work in some areas, they are now kept mainly for showing, both in harness and in-hand.

**Appearance:** The head is attractive, with a broad forehead, friendly eyes and a Roman nose. The neck is quite long and arched and set on strong, sloping shoulders. The body is deep through the girth and the quarters are rounded and strong. There is plenty of fine, silky hair on the fetlocks.

**Height:** Mares are 16 hands and over, geldings are 16.2 and over and stallions are from 17 hands upward.

**Colour:** Black, brown, bay or grey, with plenty of white on the feet and legs.

**Personality:** Shires are kind natured and very docile.

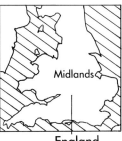

Midlands

England

▼ **Shires** are the largest heavy horses in England. Because they are handsome, as well as strong, they are popular for showing (inset).

# 4 France and The Low Countries

# Camargue

These are the wild ponies named after their homeland – the Camargue region of southern France. The Camargue's ancestry goes back a long way. They have run freely in the marshland of the Rhône delta for hundreds of years.

Selected ponies are caught and trained. Some are used by the Camargue cowboys for herding black bulls which are bred in the region. Others are used as mounts for tourist-trekking around the delta.

Camargue ponies live in herds, known as 'manèdes' (pronounced *man-ed)*. Nowadays they are rounded up regularly. Some are chosen to be broken in for training, while others are returned to live in the wild.

**Appearance:** Camargue ponies are rather shaggy and wild looking. They have straight, flat faces, and large, expressive eyes. Their short ears are set wide apart. Although their conformation is generally poor they are deep through the girth, and have powerful hindquarters. Their feet are very strong. The coat is rough and the mane and tail are long and thick.

**Height:** 13.1 to 14.1 hands.

**Colour:** Camargue foals are born black, brown or dark grey. Their coats lighten with age and, by the time they are adult, turn pale grey.

**Personality:** Because the Camargue region has extreme weather conditions, the native ponies have to be very sturdy and tough. They live on rough grass and salty water. Camargue ponies make excellent mounts when they are caught and trained. They are robust and live to an old age.

◄ **A wild Camargue pony** in his natural surroundings – the reedy, damp Rhône Delta in southern France.

# Friesian

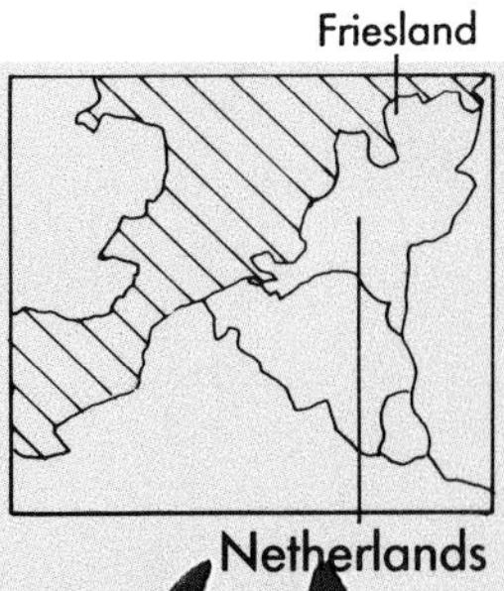

Friesians come from an area of the Netherlands called Friesland, and are one of the oldest breeds in Europe.

Although their origins lie with cold-blooded breeds, Friesians were upgraded with Andalusian and Oriental horses.

In the 18th and 19th centuries, before the days of machinery, Friesians were farm animals. Their high-stepping speedy trot also made them a popular means of transport and ideal for trotting races – an up-and-coming sport at the time.

Efforts to refine Friesians with trotter blood, in the 19th century, made them too light for farmwork and their numbers dropped. However, in recent years, great efforts have been made to preserve the breed, which is now used mainly as a carriage horse.

**Appearance:** The high-held neck and head are shapely, with lively eyes and short ears. The back and shoulders are sturdy and the quarters are well rounded. The strong legs are well-feathered.
**Height:** 15 to 16 hands.
**Colour:** Black. A small white star is acceptable.
**Personality:** Friesians are very kind-natured and easy to train.

▼ **The Dutch Friesian** is a popular carriage horse, with its elegant appearance and high-stepping trot.

Friesland

Netherlands

# French Trotter

The French Trotter was first developed in Normandy, in north-west France, during the 19th century. Its ancestors were the English Thoroughbred and the Norfolk Trotter, which were favoured for their speed and trotting ability. These were bred with native Normandy mares to produce the Anglo Norman (later known as the Selle Français) and the French Trotter. The two breeds became completely separate in the 20th century.

In 1906 a French Trotter stud book was opened. However, in the 1940s the stud book was closed to any horse whose parents had not already been registered.

Demand for trotting horses in France increased after the first trotting racecourse was opened, in Cherbourg, in 1836. Nowadays the French Trotter is bred throughout France.

**Appearance:** French Trotters vary slightly in type but they all have similar conformation. The body is deep with a strong back and shoulders and well-muscled, sloping hindquarters. The legs are long and tough.

**Height:** Up to 16.2 hands.

**Colour:** Chestnut, bay and brown are most common, but greys and roans occasionally appear.

**Personality:** These robust, elegant horses have great stamina. Their courage and willingness make them ideal for trotting races, both in harness and under saddle. They are usually raced in a sulky. This is a light, two-wheeled harness for one person. Their abilities also include jumping and general riding so, today, French Trotters are valued for breeding riding horses.

Normandy / France

▼ **The elegant French Trotter,** from Normandy, is a popular competitor in trotting races.

# Selle Français

The Selle Français is a modern breed which was established during the 20th century by merging most of France's regional breeds into one. The only other French riding horses which still have separate stud books are Arabs, Thoroughbreds, Anglo-Arabs and French Trotters.

The Anglo-Norman, reared in the famous horse-breeding region of Normandy, is the most popular foundation stock for the athletic Selle Français. As well as the Anglo-Norman, breeds such as the Limousin, Vendéen, Charentais and Angouin have played a part in its development.

The Selle Français is used for all types of riding. As well as being excellent for show jumping, eventing and dressage, some of the horses are bred for racing.

**Appearance:** Although conformation can vary, the Selle Français generally has a neat, attractive head, set on to a long neck. The shoulders are usually sloping, the chest is deep and the body is long and muscular.
**Height:** 15.2 to 16.3 hands.
**Colour:** Chestnut is most common, but can be any colour.
**Personality:** Selles Français are intelligent and steady natured.

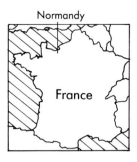

Normandy

France

▼ **The Selle Français** is a riding and competition horse produced by crossing breeds from many areas of France.

# Dutch Warmblood

▲ **Jenny Zoer** and Olympic Destiny at the 1994 World Equestrian Games.

The Dutch Warmblood is a modern breed which was first bred in the Netherlands in the 1960s due to the demand for sporting horses.

The foundation stock mares of the Dutch Warmblood were Groningen (Dutch farm horses) and Gelderland (Dutch agricultural and riding horses). These were crossed mainly with Thoroughbreds, but occasional Anglo-Arabs and Arabs were used among the breeding stallions. The Dutch Warmblood Society has laid down strict rules for breeding, and stallions are very carefully selected.

The range of horses developed by the Society is wide. They aim to breed five basic types:

**Sport horses** with excellent conformation and good movement. They are steady tempered and capable of most equestrian sports, such as show jumping, dressage and eventing. They have become one of the most successful warmbloods in the world.

**Basic riding and driving horses** are heavier than the sporting horses.

**Riding horses** are used for general-purpose riding.

**Carriage horses** are graceful, high steppers.

▲ **Hans Staub** and Dukaat ride for the Swiss team in 1994.

**Appearance:** As a whole, Dutch Warmbloods have athletic, muscular conformation.

**Height:** 15.3 to 16.3 hands.

**Colour:** Most whole colours but bays are most common.

**Personality:** Dutch Warmbloods are docile and have friendly characters.

▲ **A Dutch Warmblood** in harness for a driving competition.

**The Dutch Warmblood** has been exported all over the world to compete in equestrian sports. Limandus, ridden by Otto Hofer, represented Switzerland in the 1984 Olympic Dressage. Calypso, ridden by Melanie Smith, represented the USA at Hickstead in 1982.

# Gelderland

**Netherlands**

Gelderland

This stylish, warm-blooded breed is named after the area of the Netherlands that is its home.

Native Gelderland mares were bred with stallions from many countries, including Britain, France and Germany, to produce utility horses. They worked the land, and provided transport – both pulling carriages and being ridden.

In the 1960s, Gelderlands were important in the creation of the Dutch Warmblood, a breed of successful sporting horses. Along with the Groningen, the Gelderland was the principal foundation stock.

Nowadays Gelderlands are used for general riding and are in demand as carriage horses for competitive driving.

▼ **Gelderlands** were originally bred as utility horses, to work the land as well as provide transport. Nowadays they are put to work as carriage-driving horses.

**Appearance:** The Gelderland has a plain head with a straight, or sometimes convex (outwardly curving) face. The shoulders and body are well developed and powerful. The croup slopes slightly, with the tail high-set. The legs are relatively short but tough.

**Height:** 15.2 to 16 hands.

**Colour:** Usually chestnut, often with white markings on the face and legs. Bays, greys and occasionally skewbalds are also found.

**Personality:** Gelderlands have the ideal combination of a docile temperament and strong conformation. They are still in demand, despite the fact that they are no longer needed as workhorses. They have great presence and are ideal for showing and driving in harness. Some are ridden, and although they are not fast they can jump well.

# Groningen

The Groningen comes from a northern province of the Netherlands. It is a heavyweight warm-blood, originally bred as a farm horse. The Dutch Friesian and the German Oldenburg are its ancestors. During the 19th century the Suffolk Punch was crossed with breeding stock to give the Groningen weight and strength.

However, when machines began to take the place of horses, Groningens were inter-bred with lighter breeds to increase the tasks they could usefully do. The lightened version became a heavyweight saddle horse and, with its speed and stylish movement, a popular carriage horse.

The Groningen, along with its neighbour the Gelderland, played an important part in the development of the Dutch Warmblood, in the 1960s. The Dutch authorities have taken steps to secure the future of the breed and nowadays Groningens are popular for riding and driving.

**Appearance:** The head is long with a straight face and long ears. The Groningen has a sturdy build with powerful shoulders, a strong back and muscular quarters. Characteristic of the breed are the flat croup and the high-set tail. The legs are quite short but strong.
**Height:** 15.2 to 16 hands.
**Colour:** Black, bay and dark brown.
**Personality:** The Groningen is well known for its obedience and docile character. These qualities combined with strength and endurance ensure the continued popularity of the breed.

Groningen

Netherlands

▲ ▼ **The warm-blooded Groningen** was developed as a farm horse. It is named after the Dutch province which is its home.

# Comtois

The Comtois is a lightly built but tough draught horse from the Jura mountains, between France and Switzerland.

This cob-type breed is thought to have existed since the 6th century. In the 16th century it was famous as a cavalry and artillery horse, used during the reign of Louis XIV and by Napoleon.

Nowadays the Comtois is popular with hill farmers because it has adapted to mountainous regions and is a sure-footed worker. The farmers use the breed for transport and work in vine-yards. Comtois also pull sleighs at ski resorts and some are saddle horses.

Crosses are made between Comtois and warm-blooded breeds to produce bigger, stronger riding horses.

**Appearance:** The head is large with alert eyes and small ears. A straight neck joins the body, which is stocky and powerful with a deep girth. The back is long and straight. The Comtois has short, strong legs – with little feather – and muscular hindquarters. The mane and tail are both thick.

**Height:** 15 to 16.1 hands.

**Colour:** Varying shades of chestnut, often deepening to a dark chocolate brown or bay. In contrast, the mane and tail are light fawn.

**Personality:** Comtois are hardy and live to an old age. They are good natured, easy to train and hard work-ing. Their strength and light, quick movement made them ideal for the French cavalry.

In the 20th century the Comtois is still a popular breed, particularly in more remote areas of France where machinery has not completely taken over the role of the horse. The Comtois is also found in North Africa.

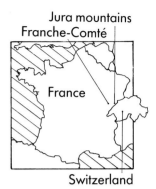

▼ **The Comtois' home** is the Jura mountains, in the area known as Franche-Comté.

This mare is typically coloured: chestnut with fawn mane and tail.

# Freiberger

The Swiss Freiberger, originally known as the Franches Montagnes, is a middle to lightweight horse, capable of agricultural and draught work.

The Freiberger is from the Jura Mountains, on the French-Swiss border, where it is still widely used today. Farmers who own land on the slopes of the mountains use these active, sure-footed horses to work the soil. The Freiberger is also popular as an artillery horse and for riding.

Nowadays the Freiberger is often crossed with Arab stock to give greater quality and make the breed lighter.

**Appearance:** The Freiberger has a small head and a cob-type body, which is stocky and compact. The legs are short and carry a little feather.
**Height:** 15.3 to 16.1 hands.
**Colour:** Most solid colours.
**Personality:** This sturdy breed is an able and willing worker as well as being intelligent and steady tempered. These characteristics make Freibergers ideal for the local Swiss farmers who rely on horses for their livelihood.

▼ **The Freiberger** is a valuable asset to mountain farmers and to artillery regiments of the Swiss army.

# Breton

Brittany, in north-west France, is the home of the Breton – an energetic, cob-type breed, which is valued by farmers for agricultural work.

There are three different types of Breton, which together meet the needs of the local people. All are descendants of the native Brittany horse. The biggest is the Draught which is bred mainly in the northern coastal area of Brittany. Its ancestors were massive horses, so the Draught is suitable for heavy farm work, pack work and transport.

The Postier Breton is a finer breed because it has warm-blooded ancestors. Bred in central Brittany, it makes a good coach horse and is capable of light farm work.

The Corlay Breton – which is now extremely rare – is the lightest of the three. In the past, its hot-blooded ancestry made it an elegant carriage horse which was also popular for riding.

**Appearance:** In general, the Breton has a broad, straight face, bright eyes and small ears. The neck is short and strong and the shoulders are sloping. The Breton has a short, muscular back and limbs, giving it great power. There is very little feather on the legs.

**Height:** The different types of Breton range from 14.3 to 16.2 hands.

**Colour:** Strawberry or blue roan, chestnut or bay.

**Personality:** The Postier is lively and good natured and makes a willing, hard worker. The Draught, like all cold bloods, has a great capacity for work requiring power and strength.

▼ **This Draught Breton** is a fine example of the breed, with its compact, well-muscled body – the characteristics which make it a 'cob-type' horse.

# Dutch Draught

This massive draught horse is one of the biggest of the European cold-bloods – it is solid muscle. The Dutch Draught is a relatively modern breed from the Netherlands, dating back about 100 years. It was developed from crossing Belgian breeds – mainly the Ardennais and the Brabant – with native Netherland horses.

In 1914 the Royal Dutch Draught Horse Society formed and, in 1925, the Society laid down restrictions to keep the breed pure. Only horses with known pedigrees can go in the stud book.

Dutch Draughts have been bred for all types of agricultural work. They can begin work when they are as young as two years old and their working lives last many years. Nowadays they are also popular for showing and breeding.

**Appearance:** The Dutch Draught has a small head, with a straight face and short ears. Its neck and shoulders are thick with muscle; the back is strong and its body is stocky. The quarters and legs are extremely powerful. A feature of the Dutch Draught is its sharp-sloping croup. The tail is low-set.

**Height:** 16.3 hands.

**Colour:** Chestnut, bay, grey, roan and black.

**Personality:** The Dutch Draught is a docile animal despite its huge size. With its steady temperament and stamina, it makes an excellent worker.

▼ **The sloping croup** of this Dutch Draught stallion is a characteristic of the breed.

# Ariège

These small, semi-wild horses are natives of the Ariège valley in the Pyrenean mountains of south-west France. They are rarely seen out of their homeland.

The Ariège are hardy, energetic and sure-footed, making them well adapted to their mountainous environment. For centuries, too, they have played an important part in the lives of local people – helping on hill farms, as carriage horses and for general riding. In recent years they have also proved popular for trekking holidays.

**Appearance:** An expressive face, short ears and alert eyes. Its neck and back are long and its shoulders are straight. The hindquarters are rounded and the legs are slender but tough. The mane and tail are luxurious.

**Height:** 13.2–15 hands.

**Colour:** Dark, usually black.

**Personality:** The Ariège are lively and hard working, but remain quite docile.

For over 2,000 years they have remained largely free from cross-breeding because their homeland is so isolated.

FRANCE

Ariège

▼ **A herd of semi-wild Ariège horses** in their mountainous homeland.

# Brabant

The Brabant (also known as the Brabançon and Belgian Heavy Draught) is a magnificent horse which takes its name from the region in central Belgium where it was first bred. This is an area where horses are known to thrive on the fertile soil and rich pasture. The Brabant dates back to the 11th century, and is believed to resemble the war horses bred in the Middle Ages.

The breed used to be prized as a draught animal because of its great pulling power. It is still a favourite in North America. Brabants have been exported all over the world for cross-breeding, to improve the quality of other heavy-horse types such as the Shire and Clydesdale in Great Britain.

**Appearance:** The Brabant is large, muscular and handsome. The head is slightly square and small in proportion to the size of the body. It has a strong neck and shoulders and massive hindquarters. The back is short and the girth is deep. The legs are strong, with plenty of feather.

**Height:** 15-17 hands.

**Colour:** Usually strawberry roan or chestnut with black points. Occasionally bay, brown, grey or dun.

**Personality:** The Brabant is a good-natured horse with a kind temperament and works willingly.

As with so many of the large draught animals, the demand for the Brabant has decreased now modern machinery is readily available. But in some of the more remote communities of Belgium the breed is highly valued.

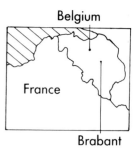

▼ **The rich grassland** of Brabant, a region in central Belgium, has played a large part in producing this impressive muscular horse. This Brabant is typically coloured — strawberry roan with black points.

# Ardennais

The Ardennais is a very ancient, cold-blooded breed. It is a willing and lively animal, as well as being immensely strong, and is ideal for all types of draught work.

Nowadays the demand for the Ardennais as a draught horse is not so great, because the work can be done by machines. However, it remains a popular sight in its homeland and many farmers keep the horses out of affection. National state studs have also been developed to preserve the breed.

Its homeland is the mountainous Ardennes region on the border of France and Belgium. But there is also a Swedish Ardennais, which has developed as a result of crossing the original Ardennais with North Swedish horses (light draught horses). The Swedish Ardennais is very similar to its French and Belgian relatives, but has the 'pony' characteristics of North Swedish horses.

The Ardennais is thought to have descended from the war horses of the Middle Ages, and was again in great demand at the beginning of the 19th century during Napoleon's invasion of Russia. More recently it was used as an artillery horse in the first World War.

**Appearance:** The Ardennais has a broad face with expressive eyes, well-opened nostrils and pointed ears. The neck is crested and the chest is wide and deep. The hindquarters are powerful and its massive body is compact. Although the legs are short, they are very muscular and well feathered.
**Height:** 15 to 16 hands.
**Colour:** Roan, grey, chestnut or bay.
**Personality:** Ardennais horses are very hardy – they can survive in unfavourable climates on little food. Despite being so tough, they are exceptionally gentle and easy to handle.

▼ **The powerful Ardennais** is an ideal draught horse. It comes from the mountainous Ardennes region, on the borders of France and Belgium.

Belgium

France

# Boulonnais

▼ **Boulonnais** are from the district near Boulogne.

France

The Boulonnais – named after the town of Boulogne, in North West France – is a powerful but elegant cold-blood.

It is set apart from other cold-blooded breeds because of the qualities it has inherited from its hot-blooded ancestors. Early in its history the Boulonnais, (pronounced *Boo-lon-ay*), was bred with Arabs and Barbs. It displays characteristics of both. For example, the Boulonnais is fast as well as strong, and is well proportioned despite its immense size.

Before the days of motorized transport, the Boulonnais was employed to pull coaches, because it could provide the power and speed needed. It was especially useful for transporting fresh fish and sea food from the coast to Paris. For this reason it earned the name 'Mareyeur' which means 'seller of fish' in French.

**Appearance:** The Boulonnais is large and heavy. Its body is deep and wide, and its back is broad. It has a short head with a straight face – the forehead is flat and its large eyes are alert. Like its hot-blooded ancestors the Boulonnais has a silky coat and luxurious, thick mane hair.
**Height:** 16–17 hands.
**Colour:** Most often shades of grey, but sometimes black, bay, red roan, blue roan or chestnut.
**Personality:** Although it is massively built the Boulonnais has a lively temperament and a very gentle nature.

In some regions Boulonnais horses are still used as farm workers, but with modern machinery and methods of transport their uses are limited. However, Boulonnais are kept at National Government-funded studs to ensure that this impressive breed does not disappear completely.

◄ **The elegant features** and head shape are due to the Boulonnais' hot-blooded ancestry.

▼ **This fine-looking breed** is massive but remains handsome and very well proportioned.

# Percheron

The French Percheron is one of the finest of today's heavy draught horses and is popular all over Europe, the USA and many other parts of the world. The Percheron's home is Le Perche, a region in northern France.

The breed's ancestors were a mixture of French and Belgian work horses, with short, sturdy legs and agile movement. They owe their fineness – unusual in a heavy horse – to Arab horses which were bred with them as far back as the Middle Ages (900-1200). Today's Percheron was first bred by a group of farmers from Le Perche, in the 1800s.

Nowadays, Percherons are often put to work on farms and, because they have strong hooves, they are used on the road for transport, too. These massive, handsome horses have also provided the foundations for other breeds.

**Appearance:** The Percheron's head is wide between the eyes. The neck is long and thick, with a broad chest and sturdy shoulders. The body is compact, with wide, muscular hindquarters. The legs are short but immensely strong, with tough hooves.

**Height:** Mares are 16.1 and over and stallions are no less than 16.3 hands.

**Colour:** Grey or black.

**Personality:** Percherons are easy to handle as they are so docile. They are efficient workers, combining strength with quick movement.

▼ **The Percheron** is a gentle giant and one of the most handsome of the heavy horse breeds. Today many Percherons can still be seen at work on the farm (inset).

# 5 Germany, Switzerland and Austria

# Dulmen Wild Pony

Germany

The Dulmen Wild Pony, which is also called the Dulmen Wild Horse, is the last remaining indigenous breed of pony in Germany. It was mentioned in documents as far back as 1316.

It is still bred today on an extensive estate called the Merfelder Bruch which is situated near Dulmen in the Westphalia region of northern Germany. The herd of about 200 animals lives in a semi-wild state.

Once a year, the herd is rounded up for an auction of yearlings – an event that attracts thousands of visitors. After the yearlings are broken in, they become riding ponies for children.

**Appearance:** The straight-faced head sits on a relatively short neck which broadens into a wide torso. The withers are not very well developed and merge into a medium length back. This robust pony has sturdy legs with small, very hard hooves.

**Height:** 12.1 to 12.3 hands.

**Colour:** Mainly dun with a darker stripe along the spine and stripes along the legs. There are also dark brown horses which have a light coloured stomach and are whitish around the muzzle.

**Personality:** This shy, half wild horse can become a loving, sweet-natured riding pony if it is treated well.

▼ **Full of life,** Dulmen ponies gallop across lush meadows near Dulmen, in northern Germany. The pony in the foreground is typically dun coloured.

# Haflinger

The Haflinger was first bred in Austria's Tyrol mountains.

Its ancestors were native, Tyrolean ponies which were bred with Arabs. The Haflinger inherited the sturdy sure-footedness of these native ponies along with the Arab's elegance.

Haflingers were originally used for pack and light draughtwork in the mountains, where today, they are popular for taking tourists on trekking holidays.

Stallions and mares which are entered in the breed's stud book are traditionally branded with an 'H' at the heart of an edelweiss – Austria's national flower.

**Appearance:** The head is slightly dished, with large eyes and small ears. Haflingers are strongly built; the chest and body are deep, the back is long and broad and the legs are tough. The mane and tail are plentiful.

**Height:** Mares 13.1¼ – 14.2 hands; stallions 13.3 – 14.2¾ hands.

**Colour:** All shades of chestnut, with a white or flaxen (light yellow) mane and tail. White markings are allowed.

**Personality:** Haflingers are hard working and long lived. They have a kind temperament and are easily handled.

Nowadays they are ridden, some are trained to jump and many are driven in harness.

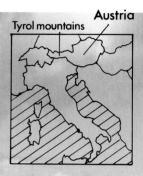

Tyrol mountains | Austria

▼ **Haflingers,** seen here in their mountainous homeland, are sturdy and sure-footed but retain the graceful lines of their Arab ancestors.

# Westphalian

Like other German warm-bloods, the Westphalian is named after a region – Nordrhein-Westfalen, in the north-western corner of West Germany. To be a Westphalian, a horse must be born in that area out of a registered mare.

The breed was popular in the 18th and 19th centuries for use by the army and on farms, and in 1826 the Westphalian Breeders' Association was set up. In the 20th century the addition of Hanoverian blood helped turn the Westphalian into a sports horse, and by the 1970s it had come to be recognized as one of the best competition horses in the world. Its first success was 'Roman', who won the 1978 World Show-jumping Championships.

Today the Westphalian is West Germany's second most popular breed (after the Hanoverian). It is used for show jumping, dressage, eventing, harness work and general riding.

**Appearance:** The Westphalian is a heavier and thicker set version of its neighbour the Hanoverian. Its head is intelligent, with a good width between the eyes. The neck is well shaped and set on to a body that is deep and broad. The hindquarters are powerful, although sometimes they can be a little flat.
**Height:** 15.2-16.2 hands.
**Colour:** Any solid colour.
**Personality:** Intelligent and bold.

Holland

Germany

Westphalia

▼ **Once a farmhorse,** the Westphalian has been developed into one of the finest sports horses in the world.

# Trakehner

The Trakehner, also known as the East Prussian Horse, was named after the Trakehnen stud in East Prussia (now part of Poland), which was started in 1732 by horse-lover King Frederick William I of Prussia.

Local Schweiken horses – small, but tough workers – were put to imported Arabs and Thoroughbreds. Before qualifying as breeding stock, the offspring of these crosses were trained as three-year-olds and tested over hunting ground as four-year-olds.

The best quality Trakehners were kept for breeding at the Trakehnen stud, while others were sent to private or state studs. Those horses that failed to meet the high selection standards were used as mounts by the Prussian army. Stallions were gelded first.

During the Second World War the Trakehnen stud was destroyed. Luckily, many Trakehners were transported to Germany, where breeding continues today.

Trakehners make excellent mounts for show jumping, dressage and eventing.

**Appearance:** Taking after the Thoroughbred, the Trakehner has a wide forehead and a narrow muzzle. The neck is long, the shoulders are sloping and the hindquarters are quite straight.
**Height:** 15.3 to 16.2 hands.
**Colour:** Usually dark, solid colours.
**Personality:** The Trakehner is spirited, like its hot-blooded relatives, but is manageable at the same time.

Germany   Poland

☐ Old Prussian Kingdom

▼ **The Trakehner** is similar to the Thoroughbred in build, but is well suited to sports such as show jumping and eventing.

# Hanoverian

The warm-blooded Hanoverian is one of the most popular of German breeds. Its origins lie with the Great War Horse of the Middle Ages, and the Hanoverian was first developed as a cavalry mount.

Great interest was taken in the breed by the English Kings, especially George II, who set up the first state stud in Germany in 1735. He sent English Thoroughbreds, Yorkshire Coach horses and Cleveland Bays to be bred with German horses. With the addition of English blood Hanoverians became successful carriage horses.

After the Second World War, the demand for leisure and sports horses increased. Hanoverians were lightened further with more Thoroughbred stock, as well as with Arab and Trakehner.

Nowadays Hanoverians are best known for dressage and show-jumping.

**Appearance:** There is a wide variety of size and shape within the breed, but generally Hanoverians have plain heads, strongly built shoulders and deep bodies. The legs and hindquarters are well made.

**Height:** 15.3 to 17 hands.

**Colour:** Most solid colours.

**Personality:** These athletic horses are intelligent and bold. They are easily disciplined and have spectacular movement. As well as excelling at dressage and jumping, Hanoverians are used for driving and general riding. Those with a lot of Thoroughbred blood are ideal for the tough sport of eventing.

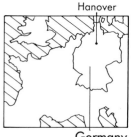

Hanover

Germany

▼ **The Hanoverian's** strong conformation and ability in most equestrian sports make it one of the most popular German breeds.

# Holstein

The Holstein is thought to be the oldest German breed. It was first bred on the richly pastured banks of the River Elbe, in the northern region of Schleswig-Holstein.

In the Middle Ages the Holstein was a heavyweight warhorse. Later, between the 16th and 18th centuries, the sturdy breed enjoyed great popularity all over Europe and many were exported.

Like the Hanoverian, the Holstein was upgraded with English stock, in particular the Yorkshire Coach Horse. It was then adapted for farmwork and carriage driving and was also used by the army.

After the Second World War the demand for workhorses fell and the Holstein was considered too heavy for most purposes. As a result its numbers fell. However, cross-breeding took place with English Thoroughbreds to lighten the horse, making it suitable for sport. Nowadays, the breed is successful at jumping, eventing, dressage and driving.

**Appearance:** The head is elegant and set on to a long neck. The back and quarters are well shaped and the legs are strong.
**Height:** 16 to 17 hands.
**Colour:** Usually bay, brown or black, but can be most solid colours.
**Personality:** Holsteins are powerful and have plenty of stamina. They are also good natured and sensible.

Compared to most other German breeds, there is only a small number of Holsteins. But they are high quality and popular for modern-day sport.

Schleswig-Holstein

River Elbe

Germany

▼ **Holsteins** have been lightened from their original size to become successful sports horses. Many have even reached Olympic level.

# Bavarian Warmblood

The Bavarian Warmblood is a sporting horse and its foundations are some of the oldest in Germany. It was first bred in the southern region of Lower Bavaria, in Germany.

The Bavarian's origins lie in the Rott Valley, also in southern Germany. The Rott valley produced the 'Rottaler' – a horse which was first a battle charger. Because of its strength it was later employed to do agricultural and draught work. By the 15th century the breed was well established.

In recent years, the Rottaler has been adapted to the needs of the time by cross-breeding. Today, through the use of lighter breeds, the Bavarian Warmblood has been developed out of Rottaler stock to provide a horse of great quality.

The German government encourages and gives financial support for such regional breeding.

**Appearance:** The body is deep, broad and very muscular, thanks to its ancestry. Because of these qualities the Bavarian is very powerful. The shoulders and legs are strong, with good, sturdy bones, making this warm-blooded horse suitable for the rigours of equestrian sport. Its tail is set high.

**Height:** Average 16.1 hands.

**Colour:** Usually chestnut, but most colours appear.

**Personality:** The Bavarian Warmblood is a good-tempered and considerate horse. Its steady, docile character, combined with its athletic conformation, make it easy to handle. It also has the skill and concentration of a top horse.

Germany

Lower Bavaria

▼ **The Bavarian Warmblood** has been developed from a work horse into an agile sporting horse. Note the mare's powerful body and the foal's athletic build.

# Swiss Warmblood

Switzerland has bred horses successfully for hundreds of years. The Swiss Warmblood was started in the 1960s and is the most recent breed to emerge from the national stud at Avenches.

The original breeding stock for the Swiss Warmblood consisted of imported Selle Français, Thoroughbred, Hanoverian, Trakehner and Swedish Warmblood stallions. They were put to imported and native mares, mainly Einsiedlers – an all-purpose breed that has now merged with the Warmblood.

For entry into the stud book, stallions are examined for good conformation, soundness, action and performance. This is usually done when they are three-and-a-half years old and again when they are five-and-a-half. The quality of their pedigrees and offspring are also taken into account. Mares are strictly tested, too.

Swiss Warmbloods make excellent mounts for general riding, competitive dressage, jumping and driving.

**Appearance:** Like most sports horses, Swiss Warmbloods have athletic conformation. The neck and shoulders are muscular, the quarters are well proportioned and the legs are strong.
**Height:** Around 16.1 hands.
**Colour:** Most solid colours.
**Personality:** Swiss Warmbloods have kind, steady natures.

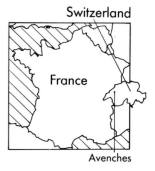

▼ **The Swiss Warmblood** is a modern sports horse with an athletic conformation. Its origins are mainly warmbloods and some Thoroughbred blood.

# Oldenburg

The Oldenburg is the tallest and heaviest of the German warm-bloods. It was originally bred in north-west Germany, in the 1600s. The Oldenburg is believed to be a relative of the Dutch Friesian.

Count Anton von Oldenburg, who gave his name to the breed, imported Spanish, Barb and Thoroughbred horses to improve local German stock.

About a hundred years later, more Thoroughbred, Cleveland Bay, Norman (French riding and carriage horses) and Hanoverian stallions were used to improve the Oldenburg. A strong horse was produced, capable of work in the fields, and in harness, as a coach horse.

After the Second World War the demand for lighter, riding horses grew.

Oldenburgs were again crossed with modern Thoroughbreds and Normans, resulting in strong riding horses that could still go in harness.

Nowadays, Oldenburgs are particularly successful in competitive driving.

**Appearance:** The Oldenburg has a plain head with a straight face. The shoulders are well made and the body is deep through the girth. The back is very strong and the hindquarters are powerful. Although it is a tall horse, the Oldenburg has relatively short legs.
**Height:** 16.2 to 17.2 hands.
**Colour:** Black, bay or brown.
**Personality:** Oldenburgs are strong and steady natured. They start work at a young age and go on for years.

▼ **The Oldenburg** is a powerful warm-blood which is popular nowadays for driving as well as riding.

# Lipizzaner

This elegant breed was developed at the Lipizza stud – which gave it its name – in the 16th century. The Lipizzaner is most famous for its appearances in the high-school dressage displays given by the Spanish Riding School, in Vienna, for the last 400 years.

The Lipizzaner's ancestors were originally bred in Spain, from Andalusian, Arab and Barb stock. Some of the best horses were imported into Austria. Here stallions were bred and trained for the art of high-school dressage, which was popular in fashionable courts.

Lipizzaners are bred along strict guidelines. Stallions are selected for their performance ability and mares for their appearance and character.

The famous Lipizzaner stud is now situated at Piber, in Austria.

**Appearance:** Lipizzaners are supremely elegant. Their heads are small and their eyes are expressive. The neck and shoulders are strong and the body is relatively long. The quarters are powerful, allowing the horse to perform difficult dressage manoeuvres.

**Height:** 15 to 16 hands.

**Colour:** Foals which have grey parents are born dark coloured. Usually they turn grey by the time they are 7-10 years old. Bays are sometimes found.

**Personality:** Lipizzaners are gifted with intelligence as well as grace. They are also docile, which makes them easy to train. Only stallions are used in the Spanish Riding School. Lipizzaners are increasingly bred in countries such as Hungary and France, where they are also used for riding and as carriage horses.

▼ **Lipizzaners** are graceful and strong. They are best known for their performances of high-school dressage with the Spanish Riding School (inset).

# Noriker

The Noriker was originally developed in the ancient state of Noricum, which was approximately modern-day Austria.

The breed has a close relative, the South German Cold-blood, which is found in Upper and Lower Bavaria. Another strain of the Noriker – the spotted Pinzgauer – was developed in the Pinzgau region of Austria, when Andalusian and Neapolitan blood were added.

Nowadays, Norikers are bred as light draught horses for work in the mountains, and used by the Austrian army. Breeding is selective and colts are tested for weight-pulling ability, as well as for the quality of their paces, before they can become stud stallions.

**Appearance:** The Noriker has a big-gish head, with a short, thick neck. The chest is deep and the back is long. The legs are short but strong and the feet are hard wearing.
**Height:** 16-16.2 hands.
**Colour:** Usually chestnut, bay or spotted, although other colours are found.
**Personality:** Norikers are sure footed and hard working. Steady by nature, they are ideal for mountain work.

▼ **The Noriker** is a sure-footed draught horse, used for work in the mountainous area of its native Austria.

# Rhineland Draught

The Rhineland Heavy Draught Horse, also known as the Rhenish Cold-Blood, was developed in the late 19th century and is named after the West German region where it originated. Its ancestors were native cold-bloods from Westphalia, Saxony and Rhineland, together with Brabants from Belgium and Ardennais horses from France. These combinations resulted in a breed which became Germany's most popular work horse.

By the beginning of the 20th century, these massive, well-muscled animals were invaluable for agriculture and heavy draught work. They were also used to breed other cold-bloods.

Though there is little demand nowadays for large draught horses, Rhinelands are still bred by enthusiasts.

**Appearance:** The Rhineland is heavily built, with a thick neck, strong shoulders and a deep, wide chest. The body is compact, the back strong and the feathered legs are sturdy.
**Height:** 16-17 hands.
**Colour:** Chestnut and red roan with flaxen or black points.
**Personality:** Like most large cold-bloods, the Rhineland is good natured and docile. Because it matures early, the breed has a long working life.

▼ **The Rhineland Heavy Draught** was once Germany's most common work horse. It is similar in build to the Brabant and the Ardennais.

# Schleswig

The Schleswig is a cobby draught horse. It is bred in the Schleswig-Holstein region, which is now part of West Germany but once belonged to Denmark. Because of this, the Schleswig has a close relative in the Danish Jutland. In the past, the two were frequently crossed.

During the Middle Ages, Schleswigs were used as saddle horses by knights who needed strong animals to carry them in their full battle armour. They were also much used as draught animals.

In the late 19th century, the Schleswig that we know today was produced by cross-breeding. The breeds most commonly crossed with Schleswigs included Bretons and Boulonnais from France.

Thoroughbreds and Yorkshire Coach Horses (now extinct) from England were also used, with the result that the Schleswig is a quick mover for its size.

**Appearance:** The head is large, with a convex profile. The chest is broad and the body is deep through the girth, with a long back. The short legs are extremely strong and have just a small amount of feather.
**Height:** 15.2 to 16 hands.
**Colour:** Most often chestnut, with a flaxen mane and tail, but it can be bay or grey.
**Personality:** Schleswigs are lively, hard-working horses.

▼ **The Schleswig** from West Germany is thick-set and very muscular. It closely resembles the Danish Jutland.

# South German Cold-blood

The South German Cold-blood is primarily bred in Bavaria, but is also found in Baden Wurtemberg and in Baden Baden, hilly regions of southern-Germany.

Its ancestors probably date back to horses of the old Roman province of Noricum and this breed has been especially favoured by the monasteries.

Over the last century, other breeds (including Cleveland Bays, Oldenburgs and Holsteins) were introduced in order to improve the quality. As a result, there now exists in the northern, most mountainous part of Bavaria a less heavy, less solid type which is called the Oberlander – its name is taken from the area from which it originates. The second type that resulted from this crossing is a heavier horse, called a Pinzgauer, which is found in the Chiemgau area.

During the last decade, attempts have been made to strengthen the breed and unify the different types within the breed. This has been done with Austrian stallions and the resulting horse, with its imposing stature, is now referred to as the South German Cold-blood.

**Appearance:** The South German Cold-blood is medium sized, and very strong and agile, with straight legs. It is well adapted to hilly as well as flat terrain and has been very useful for agricultural work.

**Height:** 15.3 to 16.2 hands.

**Colour:** Brown and bay.

**Personality:** The South German Coldblood is very even-tempered and calm. It is used in agriculture and is very popular at parades and agricultural shows, where it often demonstrates its strength by competing to pull heavy weights.

Germany

Munich

▼ **Its solid stature** and build make the South German Coldblood well adapted to alpine regions.

# 6 Scandinavia

# Gotland

The Gotland is a native of an island off the coast of Sweden, in the Baltic sea. It is thought to be the oldest of the Scandinavian breeds. Its ancestors were probably Tarpans – the dorsal stripe down the Gotland's back suggests a primitive ancestry.

At one time Gotland ponies were used for light draughtwork by farmers and as a means of transport. But when mechanization took over they became less popular.

Arab and oriental blood was introduced, and during the 20th century the Gotland improved in quality. The breed became popular again, and so many were exported that the number remaining in Sweden dropped.

However, the Swedish government stepped in and formed a society to secure the maintenance of the breed in its natural environment. Some herds still run wild in the forest on Gotland island, and many live on the mainland.

**Appearance:** The Gotland is light and elegant. Its head is small with a broad forehead, big eyes and expressive ears. The short neck and sloping shoulders are muscular and the back is quite long. The legs are strong with well-shaped hooves.

**Height:** 12 hands on average.

**Colour:** Usually bay, black, dun or palomino, but most other colours also appear. There is often a dorsal stripe.

**Personality:** Gotlands are easy to handle. Because they are agile they are good at jumping and make suitable children's mounts.

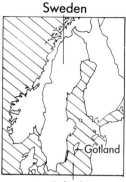

▼ **The numbers** of Swedish Gotlands are maintained by selective breeding.

# Icelandic

Iceland's hardy ponies have remained pure-bred for over 1000 years. This is because other breeds are not allowed to enter Iceland, due to the fear of importing disease.

As well as the normal walk, trot and canter, Icelandics display two other gaits, called 'tolt' and 'pace'. Tolt – also known as running walk or rack – is a rhythmic, four-time action, which is smoother than the trot. The pace is a two-time action: both legs on the same side move together, and at one point all four hooves are off the ground, giving the impression that the horse is floating.

With their unusual gaits, Icelandics take part in special gait contests, as well as dressage competitions and long-distance riding. They are also used for general riding and for gathering sheep.

**Appearance:** The head is straight with small, pointed ears and wide-set eyes. The neck is set on to firm shoulders, the chest is broad and the back is long, with a rounded barrel. A sloping croup is preferable. The mane, tail and forelock are full.

**Height:** The average is 13 hands.

**Colour:** All colours and markings.

**Personality:** Icelandics are courageous and willing workers. Although they are quite small, they are capable of carrying heavy weights, in all kinds of weather, for miles on end. They are friendly and kind with children and other animals. Because they are inexpensive to keep, and exciting to ride with their unusual gaits, they are popular all over Europe, Scandinavia and some states of North America.

Iceland

Atlantic Ocean

The British Isles

▼ **Iceland's native ponies** are pure-bred and can be any colour. They are well known for their extraordinary gaits, the tölt and the pace.

# Fjord

This unusual breed originated in western Norway and can now be found all over Scandinavia and in other countries.

Although Fjords have been domesticated for many years they still look similar to primitive horses such as Przewalski's Horse. Indeed, pictures of ponies with the same coloured coats as Fjords and similar stand-up manes have been found in Viking art, dating back some 1000 years.

Fjords are sure footed and hard working. They have been invaluable to farmers for working in mountainous regions, where tractors cannot go.

**Appearance:** The Fjord has a broad forehead with wide-set eyes and small ears. Its muscular neck is set on to a long body which is deep through the girth. The feet are hard and the legs are strong with a little feather on the fetlocks.

**Height:** 13 to 14.2 hands.

**Colour:** Most shades of dun (usually cream) with a dorsal stripe. There are often zebra stripes on the legs and the mane is a silvery colour with black hairs through the middle. It is clipped in a curve, with the dark hairs standing just above the lighter ones. The muzzle is a lighter colour than the rest of the coat and the tail and legs are usually darker.

**Personality:** Fjords are hard-working and very tough. Their docile temperaments and strength make them ideal for farmwork.

Fjords are popular for work in harness, for general riding and the modern-day, acrobatic sport of vaulting.

Scandinavia

Norway

▼ **The Norwegian Fjord** is a distinctive cream or yellow dun colour. Notice the dorsal stripe down the back, and the two-tone, stand-up mane. Note also the dark coloured legs and tail.

# Døle

The Døle is a native of the Gudbrandsdal Valley in Norway.

The Døle is very similar to the Dales and Fell. In prehistoric times, before Britain became an island, these horses were probably one and the same breed.

When pieces of land broke away from Europe and the British Isles was formed, the separate herds developed their own characteristics. In later times when trade was lively between Britain and Norway, merchants took their horses with them and crossed them with native British breeds – which therefore kept some of their original similarities.

There are two types of Døle. The first is the Gudbrandsdal: a small, tough draught animal with great pulling power and an active trot. It is still popular today for transport, packwork and farmwork over the rough ground of the valley and the surrounding land.

The second is a lighter horse: in the 1830s an English Thoroughbred stallion was exported to Norway and crossed with Gudbrandsdals to produce the Døle Trotter. Originally the Trotter was popular for light transport and later for trotting and harness races.

**Appearance:** The Trotter and the Gudbrandsdal have certain features in common: a small, pony-like head, upright shoulders, a strong, deep body, muscular quarters and a thick mane and tail. The legs are short and the heavier horses have plenty of feather.

**Height:** 14.2 to 15.2 hands.

**Colour:** Usually black, brown or bay.

**Personality:** Døles are hardy and even tempered, with a great deal of stamina. They are versatile, all-purpose horses.

Norway

Gudbrandsdal Valley

▼ **Døles are still valuable** draught animals as some areas of Norway cannot be reached by motorized vehicles.

# Knabstrup

The spotted Knabstrup, from Denmark, was developed in the 1800s and is well known for its circus appearances.

During the Napoleonic Wars Spanish troops were stationed in Denmark. When they returned home, one officer left behind a chestnut mare with a 'blanket' covering of spots.

The mare was first put to work pulling a butcher's cart, but was discovered by Major Villars Lunn, an experienced horse breeder. The Major was impressed with the mare's speed and stamina and soon bought her and placed her in his stud, named Knabstrup.

Villars Lunn developed a new breed by putting the mare to a palomino Frederiksborg. The resulting colt, with his light, metallic, spotted coat, became the foundation stallion of the modern Knabstrup breed.

**Appearance:** In recent years, breeders have concentrated on producing different coat colours and have not paid so much attention to conformation. For this reason, there is a great variety of type. However, Knabstrups are similar to their relatives, the Frederiksborgs, but are slightly more stocky.

**Height:** About 15.3 hands.

**Colour:** All spotted patterns on a roan or grey background.

**Personality:** Knabstrups are steady and enduring. These qualities make them ideal general riding horses.

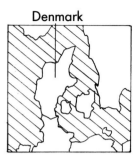

Denmark

▼ **The Danish Knabstrup**, with its striking spotted coat, is often seen in the circus.

Knabstrup is the name of the stud where the breed was developed.

# Swedish Warmblood

The Swedish Warmblood is one of today's most successful competition horses. It takes part in dressage, cross-country, show-jumping and driving events up to Olympic level.

The breed was formed to provide mounts for the Swedish cavalry. Native mares were put to Hanoverian, Trakehner, Arab and Thoroughbred stallions.

To monitor the breeding a stud book was opened and Swedish Warmbloods could enter only if they passed a rigorous examination of their conformation, character and action. Stallions also had to prove themselves in sports such as show jumping and dressage. Their off-spring underwent an inspection at the age of three to determine whether they could qualify as official breed members.

Swedish Warmbloods are exported all over the world, and are much used to upgrade other competition breeds.

**Appearance:** The Swedish Warmblood has a handsome head, with large eyes. The neck is long and the shoulders are deep. The body, quarters and limbs are all athletically built.
**Height:** 15-17 hands.
**Colour:** Can be any colour.
**Personality:** Swedish Warmbloods are intelligent and kind natured.

Sweden

Norway   Finland

▼ **The Swedish Warmblood's** athletic build makes it the ideal competition horse.

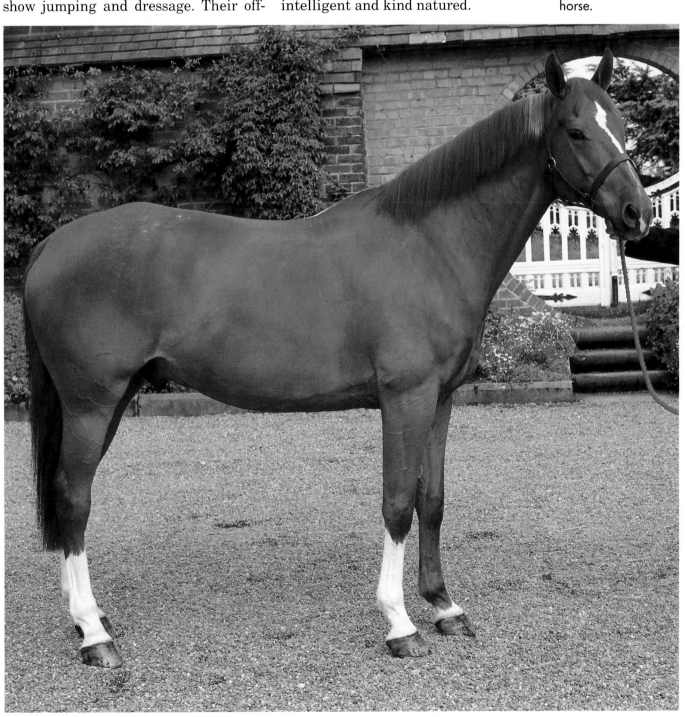

# *Jutland*

The Danish Jutland region has been the home of a breed with the same name for over 1000 years.

Denmark has a long, successful history of horse breeding. By selecting the best horses the Danes created a sturdy cold-blood with the power needed for farmwork as well as for transport.

In the Middle Ages, Danish cold-bloods were used as war horses. Their muscular build and agility made them ideal for carrying heavily armoured knights into battle.

It is believed that the Jutland is a relative of the German Schleswig and the Suffolk Punch from England. Cleveland Bays and Yorkshire Coach Horses were also used to lighten the Jutland at the beginning of the 19th century.

**Appearance:** The head is plain and is set on to a short neck. The body is deep through the chest and girth, the quarters are rounded and muscular, and the legs are short and well feathered.

**Height:** 15.2 to 16.2 hands.

**Colour:** Most often chestnut but sometimes roan or sorrel (a light reddish-brown).

**Personality:** Like most cold-bloods, the Jutland has a steady, kind temperament, coupled with strength and agility, making it ideal for working in harness and on the farm.

Denmark

Jutland

▼ **The Danish Jutland** is a hefty animal used for draught work and transport. This chestnut is about to go on the rounds, pulling a brewery dray (wagon).

# North Swedish Horse

North Sweden is the home of a robust horse that is renowned for its long life and hard-working nature. The breed has a strong constitution, and can resist most equine diseases.

The North Swedish Horse was developed by crossing native Swedish ponies with Døle horses from Norway, and later with Oldenburgs. In the early 20th century a society was formed to set standards for breeding. Nowadays stallions are tested for their work capacity before they can enter the stud book.

The breed is used for all kinds of draught work, by farmers and the army.

**Appearance:** The head is quite big, with a short, thick neck. The body is long and deep, the croup slopes and the quarters are muscular and rounded. The legs are strong. Both the mane and tail are full.
**Height:** 15 to 15.3 hands.
**Colour:** Bay, chestnut, black and dun. Dun is typical of animals with pony ancestors.
**Personality:** North Swedish Horses are bred specially for their good natures and working ability. They have an active trot that has been passed on to a lighter relative, the North Swedish Trotter.

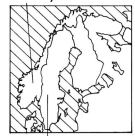

Norway

Sweden

▼ **North Swedish Horses** have muscular bodies and tough legs. Their kindly expression reflects their nature.

# 7 The Mediterranean

# Sorraia

The Sorraia pony comes from the area between the Sor and Raia tributaries of the river Sorraia, on the borders of Portugal and Spain.

The Sorraia's ancestors can be traced as far back as the Stone Age. Its colouring and primitive markings make it look rather like the ancient Tarpan. It is also thought to be related to the Portuguese Garrano – a small riding and pack pony.

Sorraia ponies are very tough: they can cope with extremes of weather and survive on small amounts of food. Before mechanization they were used for farm work and as stock horses. Nowadays, most Sorraia ponies live in the wild. One pure-bred herd, however, is closely guarded to ensure the survival of this hardy breed.

**Appearance:** The Sorraia is a hardy pony. It has a large head with a straight or slightly convex profile. Because the breed survives mainly in the wild the overall conformation is not considered to be top quality.

**Height:** 12 to 13 hands.

**Colour:** Mouse-dun with a dark stripe down the back, zebra markings on the legs and black tips on the ears.

**Personality:** Sorraia ponies are brave as well as strong.

▼ **Most Sorraia** ponies live and breed in the wild. Fine examples (inset) are specially bred to preserve the pure form.

# Alter-Real

Spain

Portugal

▼ **Note** the muscular body of the Alter-Real, which gives it power for high-stepping dressage.

The Alter-Real (pronounced *Al-tare Ray-al*) is an athletic, warm-blooded horse of high quality, popular for general riding, but best known for dressage. It was first bred in Portugal.

However, in the 19th century Napoleon led his French armies into Portugal, and during the war that followed the horses were scattered throughout Europe. The Alter-Real almost disappeared completely, but at the beginning of this century the Portuguese government took steps to restore its pure form, and the future of the breed looks secure.

**Appearance:** An elegant head, with wide-set eyes and an arched neck. The body is short and deep, with muscular hindquarters and powerful legs – the source of its high-stepping movement.
**Height:** 15 to 16 hands.
**Colour:** Bay, brown and occasionally grey or chestnut.
**Personality:** A highly strung, spirited horse, the Alter-Real is also intelligent and courageous.

# Andalusian

The Andalusian takes its name from Andalusia, the region in southern Spain where it was first bred. Because it combines graceful movement with a willing temperament, it makes a quality dressage horse. The Andalusian is also popular for general riding and often appears in festivals and ceremonies.

This noble breed has very ancient origins, and is thought to be based on native Spanish horses and hot bloods from North Africa. Its purity is due to monks who, in the 15th century, worked to prevent cross-breeding.

**Appearance:** A magnificent head is set on to a fairly thick neck, with sloping shoulders and an elegantly proportioned body. The hindquarters are broad and the legs strong. The mane and tail hair is thick and long, with the tail set low.
**Height:** 15 to 16 hands.
**Colour:** Characteristic mulberry (dappled purplish-grey) colour, as well as white, bay and grey.
**Personality:** An intelligent, proud and courageous animal, which is agile and full of fire, yet has a friendly temperament.

▼ **The handsome Andalusian,** seen here on the shores of its native southern Spain, wears a decorative harness for dressage displays.

France
Portugal
Spain
North Africa

# Lusitano

The Lusitano is an athletic breed from Portugal, and has been one of that country's top riding horses for centuries.

Although its exact origins are not known, the Lusitano is thought to be closely related to the Spanish Andalusian and the Arab.

Because of its agility and intelligence, the Lusitano was a valuable asset to the Portuguese cavalry. It was also popular with farmers who used the breed for light draught work and riding.

Lusitanos are best known in Portugal today as mounts for the *Rejoneadores* (mounted bullfighters). Portuguese bull-fighting – which does not involve killing the bull – is an exciting sport in which the horse must dodge the bull at high speeds.

Lusitanos have the talent to be skil-fully trained in high-school movements. They often give demonstrations before the bull enters the ring.

**Appearance:** The Lusitano has a small, straight or slightly convex head, similar to that of the Andalusian. The neck is quite thick and the shoulders are sloping. The body is compact and the quarters are strong. Both the mane and tail are abundant and it is not unusual for them to be wavy.

**Height:** 15-16 hands.

**Colour:** Usually grey, but often bay, black or chestnut.

**Personality:** Lusitanos have great courage as well as being alert and nimble-footed. Some are still used for light farmwork, but most are either ridden or driven.

▼ **The Portuguese Lusitano** is very similar to its relative, the Andalusian, from neighbouring Spain.

# The Arab

▲ **The distinctive shape** of the Arab's head, showing its 'dished' (inwardly curving) face.

▼ **This beautiful Arab** illustrates the graceful, flowing movement for which the breed is famous.

Of all the breeds, the Arab is possibly the most beautiful and most noble. No other horse has such a perfect combination of courage, stamina and speed, along with loyalty and gentle affection. Its hot-blooded nature and stunning good looks have been admired for hundreds of years.

By cross-breeding Arabs with horses of a more cold-blooded, docile character and heavier build, many of the world's best-known breeds have been developed.

## How it all began

The origins of the Arab are surrounded by romantic legends. According to one popular story, the prophet Mohammed wanted to select the very best horses for his warriors. He ordered his men to bring a herd of horses to an enclosure and keep them there for seven days – without water.

At the end of the week, part of the enclosure was taken down and the parched horses raced towards a nearby pool. Suddenly Mohammed sounded the battle call and five mares turned back towards him – the only horses to respond despite their desperate thirst.

All pure-bred Arabs throughout the world are said to be descended from these five mares, who showed such loyalty and devotion to their master. From that time, strict rules have been enforced to keep the blood lines as pure as possible.

Whatever their true origins, Arabs are certainly unusual – they differ from most other horses because they have 19 instead of 18 pairs of ribs.

**Appearance:** A small, 'dished' face with a broad forehead, tapering to a narrow muzzle and flared nostrils. The Arab's wide-set eyes are bright and its long ears alert. It has an arched neck, a broad, muscular chest and a strong, level back. The legs are tough and the feet are hard and round. The Arab's mane and tail hair is long, flowing and silky.

**Height:** 14.2 to 15.2 hands.

**Colour:** Most often bay, chestnut, brown or black.

**Personality:** A superb breed, famous for its intelligence and lively nature as much as for its loyalty and love of human company. Holding its head high, with mane and tail flowing, it is a picture of perfection.

The Arab is an excellent competitor, popular for endurance and racing events, as well as for general riding and showing.

➤ **Arab mare and foal.** The foal already has the alert features typical of the breed — note its bright eyes and pricked ears.

# Hot and cold-blooded horses

The terms 'hot-blooded' and 'cold-blooded' refer to temperament and not to blood temperature. Cold-bloods are docile; hot-bloods are more highly strung. Warm-bloods are a combination of the two and tend to have lively but reliable natures.

**Hot-blooded** horses are pure breeds such as Arabs and Thoroughbreds. They are fiery and full of courage. Their nervous energy makes them an ideal choice for racing.

**Cold-blooded** breeds are big draught horses like Shires and Percherons. They are steady, extremely powerful and very gentle. Because of their great strength, cold-bloods were once used for all kinds of heavy work — ploughing and pulling carts for instance. Most of this work is now done by machines, but draught horses are still a popular sight at shows.

**Warm-blooded** horses, such as the Quarter Horse and the Hanoverian, have a mixed ancestry. Their characters and looks vary according to the proportions of hot and cold blood in their breeding. Most warm-bloods combine the best qualities of both: they are good-natured, intelligent, easy to handle and athletic. For this reason, many show jumpers and competition horses are warm-blooded.

▼ **Thoroughbred.**

▼ **Shire.**

▼ **Quarter Horse.**

# Barb

The Barb is a native of North Africa and has long been associated with Morocco, Algeria and Tunisia – which make up an area once called the Barbary coast.

A lively but elegant riding horse, the Barb is also capable of speed and endurance – qualities which are seen at their best in festivals such as the North African fantasias. Barbs were once used as cavalry mounts because of their bravery and quick movement.

Many famous European breeds can trace their origins back to the hot-blooded Barb – the best-known being the Andalusian from Spain.

**Appearance:** The Barb has a straight profile and a broad muzzle. The shoulders are flat, and the chest is rounded. The hindquarters are sloping, and the legs are long and strong. Its mane and tail hair is plentiful.
**Height:** 14–15 hands.
**Colour:** Bay, brown, chestnut, black or grey.
**Personality:** The Barb is sure footed, tough and enduring over long distances, as well as being quite fast over short distances. It is an undemanding and reliable animal, despite having a spirited temperament.

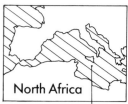

North Africa

Mediterranean Sea

▼ **North African Barbs** are noted for their elegance and hardiness. They are used in festivals to celebrate Morocco's military past.

# Italian Saddle Horse

Italy, like many European countries, is combining its regional warm-bloods and crossing them with imported stock to form one breed of sports horse – in this case the Italian Saddle Horse.

Breeding stock has been selected and imported from countries all over Europe. The Italian breeds which are being merged include:

**The Salerno**, which was developed in the 16th century with Neapolitan, Arab and Barb blood. It was popular with the Italian cavalry and has been a successful sports horse.

**The Sicilian and Sardinian Anglo-Arabs**, which have Arab and Barb ancestors, are the most popular brood mares for breeding Saddle Horses.

**Maremmanos** from Tuscany are sturdy horses which have been improved by crossing them with Thoroughbreds.

**The Sanfrantellanos** from Sicily are used for riding and harness work. They, too, have been upgraded with Thoroughbred blood.

**Appearance:** Because of the wide range of horses used to produce Italian Saddle Horses, there is a great deal of variation in appearance. However, a successful competition horse must combine strength with a relatively light build.

**Height:** 15.3 to 16.2 hands.

**Colour:** Any colour.

**Personality:** Most Italian warm-bloods are bold and intelligent. These characteristics are being passed on to Italian Saddle Horses, making them ideal for sports. Although the breed is still relatively new, the numbers are on the increase.

▼ **The Salerno** is one of the Italian warm-bloods which is being combined with imported stock to produce the modern-day Saddle Horse.

# Przewalski's Horse

In 1881 the Russian explorer Colonel Przewalski discovered the oldest breed of wild horse in the world, on the edge of the Gobi Desert. These animals had changed little in thousands of years – in fact they closely resembled the horses in drawings made by Stone Age man as long ago as 10,000 BC.

Several horses were brought to Europe, where their descendants are now thriving in captivity. Because of the risk of extinction, some horses were re-released in the mountains of Mongolia, where they now roam free.

Przewalski's Horse has a close relation, the Mongolian Horse, which is thought to be a domesticated version. Mongol tribes breed and export Mongolian Horses as foundation stock for breeds such as the China Pony, the Indian Spiti, Bhutia and Manipuri.

**Appearance:** Like the horses in the cave drawings in Europe, Przewalski's Horse has a large head, with a Roman nose, large jaw and teeth, and small ears. The body is deep with a thick neck and straight shoulders. The legs are relatively slim. The mane usually stands upright but flops over if it grows long. The tail has hair which grows in a tuft at the top.
**Height:** On average about 12 hands.
**Colour:** Dun with a black mane and tail, a mealy mouth, a dark, dorsal stripe and black, zebra-like markings on the legs.
**Personality:** Przewalski's Horses are good workers when they are domesticated.

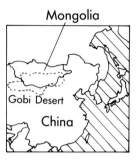

▼ **Przewalski's Horse** closely resembles horses in ancient cave drawings. The breed has changed little in thousands of years.

# Caspian

This is a breed of miniature horse, which originated in the area around the Caspian Sea and the Elburz mountains in Iran.

The Caspian has an interesting, but mysterious past. Current research shows that it may be a descendant of the native Iranian horses, which existed as long ago as 3000 BC, and that, in turn, modern-day hot-bloods may be descended from the Caspian.

For 1000 years all record of the Caspian was lost, but in 1965 these miniature horses were rediscovered along the Caspian coast.

**Appearance:** The Caspian has the proportions of a horse. Its head is fine like that of the Arab; the forehead is wide and the cheek bones are prominent. It has alert eyes, wide nostrils and a small muzzle. The neck is arched and the body is narrow with a short back. The mane and tail are silky, with the tail high–set.
**Height:** 10–12 hands.
**Colour:** Bay is the most common colour, also grey or chestnut and occasionally cream. White markings on the head and legs are accepted for showing.
**Personality:** The Caspian is intelligent and has a kindly temperament, making it ideal for children to ride. Because the Caspian is narrow, children can get their legs around its body, and so use the leg aids more easily.

Originally the breed was used for harness work, pulling carts. Nowadays it is a popular children's mount and an athletic contestant in driving competitions, despite its small size. Studs have been set up all over Europe, in Australia and New Zealand.

Caspian Sea

Iran

Elburz mountains

▼ **The Caspian** is only the height of a pony but its body has the proportions of a horse.

# Tarpan

The ancient Tarpan is claimed to be one of the first wild horse breeds. Originally it ran wild in the Ural mountains of western Russia and in central and eastern Europe.

For hundreds of years forest-dwelling Tarpans were hunted for their meat, while some were domesticated by farmers and used for light agricultural work. Sadly, by the end of the 18th century, the original breed was almost extinct, and 100 years later, in 1879, the last one is thought to have died.

A Polish professor named Vetulani took great interest in primitive horse breeds and in the early 1930s he set about restoring the Tarpan. In the Polish forests he discovered primitive ponies that bore a strong resemblance to their wild ancestors. By careful breeding, the professor managed to preserve their characteristics and create the modern-day Tarpan. Today there are several herds living a natural existence on a government-owned reserve in Poland.

**Appearance:** The head is long and broad, with a convex profile. The neck is short and thick, and the shoulders are sloping. The quarters slant toward a high-set tail.

**Height:** About 13 hands.

**Colour:** From mouse dun to shades of brown, with a dark dorsal stripe. There are black zebra markings on the legs and sometimes on the body.

**Personality:** Like their wild ancestors, Tarpans are brave.

▼ **The modern-day Tarpan** was carefully bred from Polish forest ponies very similar to the ancient breed.

# Viatka

The Viatka comes from the area along the River Viatka, in the Udmurt and Kirov regions of Russia. Like its relatives, the Polish Konik and the Estonian Klepper, the Viatka is a primitive type of pony and has the typical characteristics of strength and stamina.

With its thick coat and layer of fat under the skin, the Viatka can survive in very cold climates. It has long been popular for light farm work and, harnessed three abreast, for pulling the Russian sleigh known as the *troika*. It is also used under saddle.

The Viatka has remained almost purebred for hundreds of years. In an attempt to preserve it in this form, breeding is now strictly controlled in state studs.

**Appearance:** The head is quite long, with a broad forehead and a large lower jaw. The neck is long, the withers are high and the shoulders are muscular and sloping. The chest is deep and the back is long and broad. Both mane and tail are full.
**Height:** 13-15 hands.
**Colour:** Palomino, chestnut or dun, with a dark dorsal stripe and often zebra markings on the legs.
**Personality:** The Viatka is energetic and easy to handle.

▼ **The Russian Viatka** is a primitive type pony. A good all-rounder, it is ridden and used in-harness.

# Nonius

This sturdy breed was originally started at the Mezöhegyes stud in Hungary during the Napoleonic wars at the end of the 18th century. The foundation sire was a French Anglo-Norman, named Nonius who was captured from a French stud by the Hungarians.

Nonius covered a variety of mares, including Arabs, Holsteins and Lipizzaners. These crosses were the beginning of the Nonius breed, and produced carriage, light-draught and riding horses. They were popular with the Hungarian army and with farmers.

In the 19th century Nonius mares were crossed with Thoroughbreds. Their offspring were a lighter variety of Nonius which have become popular sports horses.

**Appearance:** Although Nonius vary in height they are generally of a similar type. The head is attractive, with an arched neck and sloping shoulders. The back is broad, the hindquarters are well muscled and the limbs are strong.

**Height:** The lighter type ranges from 14.3 to 15.3 hands; the heavier from 15.3 to 16.2 hands.

**Colour:** Black, brown or bay. White markings are quite common.

**Personality:** Nonius are sensible and easy to handle. They are slow to mature and do not start working until they are four or five. Their working lives, however, last many years.

▼ **The Hungarian Nonius** varies in height, but generally has sturdy conformation and an even temperament.

# Toric

The Toric is a cobby warm-blooded breed of horse that was developed in Estonia during the 19th century. Until its appearance, local farmers had used native ponies called Kleppers for all types of work.

In an effort to upgrade the Kleppers, mares were bred with a Norfolk Roadster stallion called Hatman, who was exported from England to Russia in 1894. These crosses formed the basis of the new breed, to which Orlov Trotter, East Friesian, East Prussian (later known as Trakehner), Hanoverian, Arab, Thoroughbred and Ardennais blood was added. By 1950 the Toric was an officially recognized breed.

There are two different types of Toric: a light riding horse with the ability to jump, and a slightly heavier, energetic workhorse used in-harness.

**Appearance:** The head is medium sized, with expressive eyes and wide nostrils. The neck is well muscled, with broad withers set on to a straight back. The quarters are powerful and so are the short, lightly feathered legs.
**Height:** About 15 hands.
**Colour:** Usually chestnut or bay.
**Personality:** Torics are steady natured and well suited to all kinds of work.

▼ **The Russian Toric** is an efficient workhorse breed that is also ridden and jumped.

# Akhal-Teké

This stunningly coloured horse was first ridden 2,500 years ago by horse herdsmen of the desert lands around the Caspian Sea. It is still bred in the area today.

**Appearance:** A distinctive and elegant breed with a beautifully shaped head, expressive eyes and long ears. The Akhal-Teké has a slender neck and a long body with sloping quarters. The legs are strong and the feet large. Its mane and tail are fine and silky.

**Height:** Between 14.2 and 15.2 hands.
**Colour:** Famous for its light, honey-gold coat, which has a metallic sheen. Bays and silvery greys are also known.
**Personality:** A spirited animal, the Akhal-Teké is hardy and has great stamina. Because of its suppleness and versatility, it makes a top-class riding horse and excels in competitive events such as jumping and dressage. It is also a prized race horse.

▼ **The hot-blooded** Akhal-Teké is one of the world's oldest breeds. It is an excellent riding horse and is highly valued in its native Russia.

Caspian Sea
Black Sea
Turkey
Iran

# Budyonny

The Budyonny (also known as Budenny) was first bred in Russia in the 1920s and is now a valued sporting horse. It is named after Marshal Budyonny, a cavalry officer and hero of the 1917 Russian Revolution.

After the Second World War, Marshal Budyonny encouraged strict breeding patterns, to create a quality cavalry horse. English Thoroughbreds and Russian Don horses were selected and crossbred to produce the perfect military mount – a horse with speed, steady nature and endurance. By 1948 it was a recognized breed worldwide.

Nowadays, Budyonnys are bred in government-controlled studs in the southern Rostov region of Russia. They are reared in large herds and live a semi-wild existence.

**Appearance:** The Budyonny has excellent conformation for an athlete. The head is attractive, the body is deep and the hindquarters are well developed. Its legs are long and fine, with the hindlegs providing the power to meet the demands of equestrian sport.

**Height:** 15.2 to 16 hands.

**Colour:** Most often chestnut but sometimes bay, brown or black. As with many of the Russian breeds the Budyonny's coat often has a golden sheen.

**Personality:** The Budyonny is intelligent and willing. Both of these characteristics, along with its excellent build, have helped make it a popular horse for competitive sports. It is particularly good at eventing, dressage, steeplechasing, show jumping and long-distance riding.

▼ **The Russian Budyonny.** A fine example of this athletic, modern breed, which was first bred in the 1920s.

# Don

The Don is a Russian breed which was first used by the Cossacks from western Russia.

The Don – developed by crossing native horses with larger Russian and Iranian breeds – was bred by Cossacks living on the dry, grassy plains around the Don and Volga rivers. Conditions here are harsh – with bitter winters and searing hot summers – so the horses must be tough and adaptable.

This background proved its worth when, in 1812, the Dons were involved in a famous battle. Napoleon's army had reached Moscow itself and the French seemed certain to conquer Russia as a result. But Cossack units forced Napoleon to retreat and then went on to drive his army all the way back to Paris. The Russian winter took a heavy toll of the exhausted French cavalry but the hardy Dons survived both the long journey and the terrible weather.

In the 19th century, the introduction of Thoroughbred and Arab blood gave the Don height and elegance without reducing its natural hardiness. With this upgrading, no further crosses were necessary. Today the Don is pure-bred.

**Appearance:** The Don is lean and elegant. Its head is similar to that of the Thoroughbred: it is broad between the eyes, with small ears. The neck is long and straight with an upright shoulder. Its body is long and deep and the legs are long and strong.
**Height:** 15.1 to 16.2 hands.
**Colour:** Chestnut, bay or grey, sometimes with a golden sheen to the coat, which is common in Russian breeds.
**Personality:** Dons bred in the wild developed great stamina. They can go for long distances and withstand extreme weather conditions. They are popular today for endurance and general riding, and as foundation stock for other breeds, for example, the Budyonny.

▼ **The elegant Don** was developed by the Russian Cossacks. Their homeland is the dry, grassy plains around the Don and Volga rivers.

# Hungarian Half-bred

Austria Hungary

Italy

Yugoslavia

▼ **Furioso** stock provided the foundation for the Mezöhegyes half-bred.

Hungary is famous for horse breeding. A half-bred can be a horse with one warm-blooded parent and one English Thoroughbred, or pure-bred Arab, parent. Hungarian half-breds were originally developed to provide cavalry mounts and to be used for light agricultural work. There are three types:

**The Mezöhegyes** stud has produced a half-bred of the same name, from Furioso/North Star stock. The Furioso's foundation sires were an English Thoroughbred called 'Furioso' and 'North Star', a Norfolk Roadster (trotter). Since the early 1960s Holstein and Hanoverian blood has been added to improve the breed, which is now known as the Mezöhegyes half-bred.

**The Kisber,** named after the stud where it was developed, is the lightest of the three. German blood was the foundation stock, but the addition of Thoroughbred blood has improved the Kisber for eventing.

**The Gidran,** named after the Arab sire 'Gidran Senior', is an Arab-type half-bred. Arab and native-mare crosses were made and later Thoroughbred and more Arab blood were added.

**Appearance:** Hungarian half-breds vary in size and shape. Generally they are well built, with strength in the shoulders and hindquarters.

**Height:** From 15.3 to 16 hands.

**Colour:** Usually any solid colour.

**Personality:** The Mezöhegyes is an ideal riding horse and is capable of most sports, as is the Gidran. Hungarian half-breds are probably best known for their success as competitive carriage driving horses.

# Kabardin

The Kabardin originated in the northern Caucasus mountains of the USSR, and is thought to have existed for about 400 years. The breed was developed by crossing native steppe horses with Russian Karabakhs, Persian horses and Turkomans from north Turkey.

Kabardins are well adapted to cope with the mountainous terrain of their homeland – they have strong legs and feet and are docile by nature. They are best known for their ability to travel for long distances over narrow, winding tracks and are still used by nomads today as pack horses and for general riding.

Since the beginning of the 20th century Kabardins have been crossed with Thoroughbreds to make them more elegant and give them more speed.

**Appearance:** The head is narrow and the ears tend to curve inward. The neck is short but muscular and the shoulders are straight. The back is relatively short and the croup is sloping. The legs are short but tough and the feet are sound.
**Height:** 14.2 to 15.1 hands.
**Colour:** Bay, dark brown, black or grey.
**Personality:** Kabardins are hardy and have plenty of stamina, enabling them to cope with long, hazardous journeys they make through the Caucasus mountains. The Thoroughbred in modern-day Kabardins makes them ideal for racing and local equestrian games.

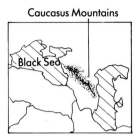

Caucasus Mountains

Black Sea

▼ **The Russian Kabardin** is well known for its ability to cope with the hazards of ridden and pack work in the Caucasus mountains.

# Karabair

The Karabair is from the mountains of Uzbekistan in central Asia, an area which has been famous for horse breeding for over 2000 years.

The breed's exact origins are unknown but it is thought to be a relative of the Arab because it looks like a stockier version. Mongolian and native steppe horses and breeds from Iran and Turkey are also believed to have been used in developing the Karabair.

Karabairs are adaptable to different disciplines. Some are used for riding and driving in harness, while heavier types work on farms.

Modern-day breeding of Karabairs has included crosses with Thoroughbreds, to produce horses capable of competitive sports, such as jumping and eventing.

**Appearance:** The Karabair is similar in looks to the Arab, but it is less refined. The head is either straight or slightly convex, the neck is straight and thickset and the back is short and strong. The croup is round and the legs are short but tough. There is little mane and tail hair.

**Height:** About 15.1 hands.

**Colour:** Grey, chestnut and bay are most common, but other colours are found.

**Personality:** Karabairs, like most mountain horses, are tough and enduring. They are also spirited, which is an indication of their Arab ancestry.

▼ **The Karabair**, from Uzbekistan, is similar in build and temperament to the Arab, which is thought to be one of its ancestors.

# Orlov Trotter

The Orlov Trotter was started by Count Orlov, in Russia, in 1777. For many years the breed was the best-known trotting horse in the world.

The original stallion was an Arab called Smetanka who sired a colt named Polken. Polken was in turn put to a Dutch mare and sired the founding Orlov stallion named Barrs.

Trotting races were popular in Russia by the 1790s; the first were held in Moscow. Orlovs were bred primarily for racing although they were also used as saddle horses and for pulling troikas (three-horse carriages or sledges).

However, when the American Standardbred was developed in the 19th century, the Orlov was no longer the fastest trotter. As a result, some Orlovs were crossed with Standardbreds and their offspring became known as Russian Trotters.

**Appearance:** The Orlov has an Arab-like head. Its shoulders are straight but muscular, the chest is broad and the body is deep through the girth. The back is relatively long and the croup and quarters are powerful. The legs are particularly strong.

**Height:** 15.2 to 17 hands.

**Colour:** Grey and black are most common, but bays and chestnuts are found.

**Personality:** Orlov Trotters are tough and enduring. They live for a long time. They are still raced today, but many are also used as foundation stock and for upgrading other breeds.

Moscow

Russia

▼ **The Orlov Trotter** was once the world's foremost trotting horse. Nowadays, the Orlov's strength and stamina mean it is widely used for adding quality to other breeds.

# Shagya

The Shagya is a Hungarian version of the Arab. Its origins lie with an Arab stallion of the same name, who was foaled in Syria in 1830. Shagya was bought by the Hungarians and taken to the Babolna stud, where he was put to native Hungarian mares of Arab descent.

Over the years careful selection of stock, as well as in-breeding of the off-spring, has produced a small but tough horse with the endurance, elegance and grace of its hot-blooded forefathers.

Shagyas were developed principally as cavalry mounts. Nowadays, they are mainly bred for sport and general riding. Many have been exported.

**Appearance:** Shagyas are very similar in build to Arabs, but they tend to be a little more thick-set.
**Height:** 14-15 hands.
**Colour:** Usually grey, but can be all the Arab colours.
**Personality:** The Shagya is a hardy courageous horse with great stamina.

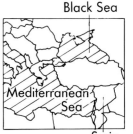

▼ **The Shagya** is not quite a pure-bred: its origins have a strong Arab influence.

# Tersky

The main foundation stock for the Tersky was the Russian Strelet – a breed similar to the Arab. The Strelet was in grave danger of extinction, and in an attempt to preserve its fine qualities, the last remaining Strelets were taken to the Tersk stud at Stavropol, in the northern Caucasus mountains of the USSR. There they were mated with pure-bred Arabs, Kabardins and Dons.

By 1948 the Tersky had emerged as an official breed and taken the name of the stud. It inherited many of the characteristics of the Strelet and was enduring, athletic and very tough.

Today the breed is raced against Arabs, ridden in endurance competitions and used in harness by the army. It also appears in the circus and is widely used to upgrade other horses.

**Appearance:** The Tersky's head is medium-sized and set on to a long neck. The shoulders are sloping and the back is long. The body is deep through the girth and the quarters are broad.
**Height:** 14.3 to 15.1 hands.
**Colour:** Most often grey, but they can also be bay or chestnut.
**Personality:** Terskys are good natured.

▼ **The Tersky** is lithe and elegant. Like its extinct relative the Strelet, the Tersky has great powers of endurance.

# Wielkopolski

The Wielkopolski is one of Poland's best known breeds. Its foundation stock was a mixture of the two Polish saddle-horse breeds, the Poznan and the Mazury, both of which came from the Trakehner.

Originally bred for draft work on farms, the Wielkopolski has also proved a capable sports horse and often does well at international competitions. Today Wielkopolskis are bred at 13 Polish state studs as well as on private farms.

**Appearance:** The Wielkopolski is a strong, middle to heavy-weight horse. It has muscular legs and short cannon bones, making it a useful riding horse. Its head looks intelligent and is set on to a well-shaped neck.
**Height:** 16-16.1 hands.
**Colour:** Usually chestnut, but can be bay, black or grey.
**Personality:** The Wielkopolski is gentle, courageous and sensible.

Poland

▼ **The Wielkopolski** is excellent for both riding and driving.

# Kladruber

The Kladruber takes its name from the Kladruby stud near Pilsen, in the Czech Republic. Kladruby was founded in the 16th century and is the oldest working stud in the world. Its aim was to develop coaching horses for use in the reigning Emperor's court.

The first horses to be imported to the stud were Spanish Andalusians. They were bred with Barbs, Turkish and native horses and were ancestors of the modern-day Kladruber. The Lipizzaner also played a part in its development.

By the end of the Second World War the number of Kladrubers had fallen. Steps were taken to encourage breeding and give the horse more substance. Crosses were made with Oldenburgs, Anglo-Normans (French Saddle Horses) and Hanoverians.

Nowadays Kladrubers are bred in two colours: grey and black. Greys are produced at Kladruby itself and blacks at a neighbouring stud.

**Appearance:** The Kladruber is similar in looks to the Andalusian and the Lipizzaner. The face is convex with bright eyes. The powerful, crested neck is set on to sloping shoulders and a long body. The quarters and legs are strong.
**Height:** 16.2 to 17 hands.
**Colour:** Grey and black.
**Personality:** Kladrubers are kind tempered as well as intelligent. The combination of their strength and steady natures make them ideal carriage horses. In addition to driving, Kladrubers are used for farmwork and for breeding riding horses.

The Czech Republic
Pilsen
Slovakia

▼ **The Kladruber** is a strong, noble horse, which was developed for driving.
The first Kladrubers were bred at Kladruby, the oldest working stud in the world.

# Vladimir Heavy Draught

The Vladimir Heavy Draught Horse is a modern breed from the region of Vladimir, near Moscow.

At the end of the 19th century many English and French breeds were imported to the USSR to develop a new workhorse. Among them were Cleveland Bays, Suffolk Punches, Clydesdales, Shires, Ardennais and Percherons. After many years of careful breeding with native mares, the Vladimir Heavy Draught emerged in 1950.

It is the perfect worker: docile and kind, it matures at an early age, and its enormous strength makes it suitable for all types of farm and draught work. Some are used to pull Russian troika sleighs.

**Appearance:** The Vladimir is cob-like – its head is large with a Roman nose. The neck is long and muscular, the back is broad and the croup is sloping. The legs are strong and feathered.
**Height:** 15-16 hands.
**Colour:** Most often bay, but Vladimirs can be any solid colour.
**Personality:** The Vladimir is lively but manageable and friendly.

▼ **The Vladimir Heavy Draught** has cobby features and the docile nature of its larger ancestors.

# 9 Using the Breeds and Types

# At work in the outback

In many parts of Australia, horses are used for herding and getting around the vast areas of each station. Horses cope well on rough terrain and are also skilful at managing temperamental cattle.

## Hard work

Station work makes many demands on stock-horses and their riders. The cattle have to graze over a wide area because vegetation in Australia is sparse, and rounding them up can take as much as two months. The horses need staying power to cope with the

▲ **Horse and rider** must work as a team. When it comes to calf-roping, the horses are trained to react quickly.

➤ **Stockhorses do not** need to wear shoes but their hooves are checked regularly, and trimmed before setting off for work.

long rides, and must be hardy as they feed on grass alone. In the winter, their diet is supplemented with hay.

Tough feet are essential as the horses work unshod. While the riders concentrate on the task in hand, they rely on their horses to be sure-footed and to look out for potholes.

Working stockhorses must also be brave enough to enter a herd of sometimes frightened cattle. The young steers, as they are called, are almost wild and hardly ever handled. As a result, they are difficult animals to herd.

A stockman rides in a Western style which is suited to long-distance travelling. Kneepads and long stirrups also help to make a tiring day in the saddle more comfortable. The thin reins are held in one hand and the horse is directed by neck reining; together with the usual leg aids, the rider moves the reins across the horse's neck in the direction he wants to go.

The horses are trained to obey the subtlest of instructions and to react with the minimum of guidance. Stockmen look for a mount with an even temper. Horses that have developed 'cow sense' and can anticipate a steer's next move are highly prized.

## Special manoeuvres

One task a stockhorse may be asked to do is to 'separate out' a steer. Sometimes an animal has to be singled out from ➤

### ★ BREEDS BROUGHT IN

The horse is not native to Australia, but was brought over by settlers. The first horses arrived by ship on January 26, 1788 and, although there are no surviving records, they were believed to be a stallion, four mares and some fillies.

Regular shipments of a variety of breeds followed – Arabs, Barbs and Basuto ponies from Africa as well as Thoroughbreds and draught-horse breeds from England.

Another horse brought over was the American Quarter Horse which came from Eastern America. Its name arose because it was tested in races over a quarter of a mile.

◄ **The Australian stockhorse, the Waler**, is the result of cross-breeding. It stands between 15 and 16 hands high and is light-framed but strong. The breed is named after the Australian State of New South Wales where it originated.

## FOLKSONGS AND FREEDOM

Australia's wild horses, the Brumbies, are descended from those used by the early settlers.

Some horses ran away from the ranches, or were set free when their owners no longer needed them.

There are few Brumbies left in the wild today. But if people want to catch one, salt is used as bait because it is in short supply in the wild.

Popular folksongs have lyrics about the freedom of the Brumby ponies, like this verse from a song called 'Brumby Jack':

'See the dust cloud on the plain,
    Hear the sound like falling rain,
    Flashing hooves and heads held high,
    As the wild bush Brumbies gallop by.

'... From the mountainside to the distant plain,
    Here and there and back again,
    They roam the country wild and free,
    'Cause that's the way they want to be.'

➤ **The rough pasture** where cattle in Australia graze makes the horse essential for getting about when it comes to round-up time.

Dogs help with the work; here they are following the horse's tracks so they can make their way through the tall spear grass!

a herd to be inoculated or put into quarantine if it is sick.

Isolating the steer is done by a highly skilled manoeuvre called 'cutting in'. Two stockmen work as a team; their horses are trained to run together, keeping the steer sandwiched between them. One rider then throws a lasso over its neck while the other rider brings the animal down by lassoing the legs.

A good stockhorse is also trained to stand still if its reins are dropped. This is essential as there is little chance to tie horses up in the outback.

Cowboy films give a false impression of what ranch life is like. Cattle herding involves little galloping; the cattle would stampede and lose too much weight in the process. The whole object is to keep the cattle happy and get them to retain their weight as they travel.

► **Over long distances** it's important to know where the horses can be watered.

▼ **In such wide open spaces,** cattle herding is skilled work. One stockman leads the herd while others stay at the back to keep the cattle under control and watch out for strays lagging behind the rest.

# The horsemen of Mongolia

In Mongolia, life without horses is hard to imagine. There are more horses than people in this Central Asian country, which lies between China and Russia. The Mongolians are traditionally nomadic people, and the horse has always been essential to them.

## A history of horses

Horses have been used for centuries to herd sheep and goats and to round up livestock which includes herds of camels. The herdsmen train their horses to manoeuvre as nimbly as sheepdogs.

The Mongolians value horses highly and, in their animal currency, one horse is equal to seven sheep, 14 goats or half a camel.

## Domestic and wild

Mongolian horses are a distinct breed. They have a smooth shuffling gait, a pace between a walk and a canter. There are two kinds, the domesticated (used by the herdsmen) and the wild horses.

The domesticated horses stay outdoors throughout the year, living in herds. In the spring they break up into groups of ten to 30 mares, guarded by a stallion. The horses would refuse to enter a stable, since none of them have ever seen, or lived under, a roof! They are not given names and are never kept as pets: theirs is simply a working relationship with their masters.

But the herdsmen look after their horses well: they let them roam freely near the camps because the animals

▼ **The horses** live in herds until they are needed for riding. When a horse is taken out of the herd, the horseman catches it by using a leather loop attached to the end of a birch pole which is 4.5m (15ft) long.

need large areas of grazing to feed on. If in some parts there is not enough grass, the hardy breed is able to live on bushes normally eaten by the camels.

Wild Mongolian horses are dun with black manes and tails. They are smaller and more heavily built than the domesticated horses. Efforts are being made to re-introduce wild herds to different parts of the country, but they are very shy and wary of new places.

On their own, both types know how to take care of themselves in the harsh climate. This is a region with extremes of temperature. When the weather turns cold they head for higher ground where snow provides a water source. These strong horses can survive conditions other breeds would find intolerable.

## The riders

Mongolian herdsmen do not shoe their horses, except in mountain areas. Mongolia has few roads, and most of the travelling is done over rough tracks. The horses can cover up to 96km (60 miles) in a day. After two days of travel at such an intensive stretch, a horse is given two weeks of rest.

The riders carry short stubby whips, and wear felt boots without heels. They ride in small wooden-framed saddles with flat stirrups. The saddle is lined

▼ **In Mongolia**, even the tamed horses lead a semi-wild existence. During the breeding season, stallions fight jealously.

166

**DID YOU KNOW?**
There is a popular saying that sums up how much the Mongolians rely on horses: 'The Mongol first learns to ride a horse and only then to walk'.

▼ **Domesticated horses** can be all colours – grey, chestnut, bay or sorrel (reddish-brown). Many patterns have been introduced through cross-breeding with horses from neighbouring Russia.

with felt padding underneath to make it more comfortable for the horse.

On festival days when the horsemen want to look special, they tack up with ornate saddles that have felt-lined panels, studded with silver.

## Children's festival

Horse racing is a national sport in Mongolia. Only children take part in the annual races, held on 11 July, Mongolia's National Day. An 'instant' city, made up of hundreds of tents, springs up on the outskirts of the capital. People come from all parts of the country to watch and take part in the racing.

Sometimes there are more than 1300 entrants for the races. The classes divide into six different age groups: the youngest horses are aged two and race across 15km (9 miles), while the oldest, aged 12, race twice the distance. No special tracks are prepared and the mountainous course includes ravines and steep hills.

The riders line up at the starting line, forming circles and singing to cheer themselves and their horses on. On the back of their brightly coloured clothes are pictures of falcons and butterflies, that suggest their horse's swiftness. Ornaments also embellish the horse-cloth and even the brushes used for grooming.

The winners are handed small bowls filled with *koumiss*, a drink made from mare's milk. They pour some of it over their horses' heads and cruppers before draining the bowl themselves. Afterwards there is a ceremony to award the winners their medals.

▼ **Children** line up in trials, hoping to be selected for races that take place annually on Mongolia's National Day. The bridles are simple in design and stitched by hand.

▼ **This young rider** shows typical confidence in the saddle. The horse's tail is tied to keep it out of the way. Despite the poor conformation of the domesticated horses, they are strong and wiry.

▼ **Big leap over:**
The sheer size of the
fences makes the
National the most
dramatic of jump
races.

# The Grand National

The boldest sport Thoroughbreds are used for is steeplechasing. From the mid-18th century in England, open fields were enclosed by fences and hedges that had to be jumped over on a day's hunting. Riders wanting to test whose 'leaper' or 'chaser' was the fastest began to hold races between the most obvious fixed local landmarks – church steeples.

### Four to a bed!

Races like these became known as 'steeplechases', and the most dramatic of them all was the Grand National. It was first run at Aintree near Liverpool in 1839 and attracted such crowds that hotel guests were sleeping four to a bed!

The field of 17 rode just over 6km (4 miles) across ploughed fields, taking in small banks, a couple of sheep hurdles and three massive fences – a wall and two brooks.

Today, the Grand National takes place at the Aintree racecourse each spring and is mostly run by professional jockeys.

### Lucky streak

Although fitness, stamina and 'heart' are vital qualities for a National winner, this is one race where luck plays as important a part as form.

The most improbable horses have made their way to the winner's enclosure – and some of the best ones have unexpectedly failed to win. The author Dick Francis was a top jockey before he turned to writing horsy thrillers. He was riding a tremendous Grand National finish in 1956 when his horse suddenly jumped a phantom obstacle. The horse's legs gave way on 'landing' and he fell – much to the disappointment of his owner, the Queen Mother.

In 1967 an outside horse, Foinavon, scooped a victory because he was the only mount far enough behind a 28-horse pile-up not to be put off by the disaster!

### Unlikely winners

Some horses became legendary winners against seemingly huge odds. When Red Rum was bought for a bargain price at the Dublin sales, he looked at first sight to be chronically lame. Yet he went on to win the Grand National three times – in 1973, 1974 and 1977 – and also holds the course record of 9 minutes 1.9 seconds.

The 1981 race produced another great win. Bob Champion rode Aldaniti to one of the most emotional and popular victories in Aintree history. Aldaniti's racing career seemed wrecked by tendon trouble, while Bob Champion had just overcome cancer. Bob's winning wish was that people would realize there is always hope, and that all battles can be won.

### Tough on the turf

A horse has to be brave, honest and sure; he has to clear 30 huge jumps, and gallop round a punishing 7km (4½ miles) course as well. This is about 1.5km (1 mile) longer than ➤

► **The first** steeplechase was said to be in 1803 when young officers dared each other to a moonlight race. They rode in nightcaps, with pajamas over their uniforms.

other jump race distances.

The race goes twice round the Aintree circuit: there are 16 jumps the first time round, but two are left out on the second round – The Chair and the Water Jump.

There can be up to 40 horses riding the Grand National field, and riderless horses galloping to the finish make the run specially hazardous.

## Sport of enthusiasts

Unlike flat racing, steeplechasing is not greatly profitable for jockeys, trainers or owners. There's more love than money in this sport. Prize money for the leading flat race, the Derby, is five times

◄ **The horses** gather for the start. Until recently, only horses who had won a certain amount of prize money could qualify to run.

greater than the Grand National. But there is more than one prize at Aintree: the winner's groom and the groom of the best turned-out horse each receive cash and a carriage clock to treasure.

## Women jockeys

Several women riders have ridden the Grand National and Geraldine Rees entered the record books as the first to complete the run: she rode in eighth on Cheers in 1982.

The world is still waiting for an equestrian heroine to romp home first, just as Velvet Brown did in Enid Bagnold's classic story, 'National Velvet'.

▼ **In most races,** the aim is to get round the course and win; for the National just getting round is a challenge in itself!

## Champion line-up

◄ **Red Rum** is a legendary champion and holds the record for the fastest time round the Grand National course. By 1977, when he was 12 years old, he had raced more than 90 times and cleared 150 Aintree fences without falling once.

► **The last fence** in the Grand National when the Thoroughbreds Moorcroft Boy (leading) and Minnehoma (eventual winner) fight it out for one of the greatest prizes in the world of sport. Champion jockey Richard Dunwoody rode Minnehoma who was trained by Martin Pipe.

◄ **Corbière** won the National in 1983, yet as a youngster he seemed an unlikely future champion — he had the lolloping gallop of a baby elephant! His potential was spotted when he was turned out to summer grass as a five-year-old. He kept bounding fences to reach the filly in the next field! Jenny Pitman took Corbière on and became the first woman to train a Grand National winner.

# The finest of fences

Building the perfect Aintree fences takes eight months from start to finish. Some of the fences have taken root on the course because they have been there so long. Their core is sturdy thorn, and the prickly branches are covered over with soft brush a month before the race. It takes 20 lorry loads to do the job!

The take-off side of the fence is sloped upwards to give the horses a better chance of clearing the top-most brush. Before the race, experts check all the fences to make sure horses and jockeys are not at risk. Television microphones are hidden safely inside each jump so that those who watch the race at home can hear the sound of thundering hooves.

Canal Turn: 150cm (5ft) high and 99cm (3ft 3in) wide. The horses make a 90-degree turn to the left immediately after this jump

spruce fence 147cm (4ft 9in) high and 90cm (3ft) wide

lake

gorse fence 150cm (5ft) high and 90cm (3ft) wide

Valentine's Brook: 150cm (5ft) high and 165cm (5½ft) wide, including a ditch

gorse fence 150cm (5ft) high and 165cm (5½ft) wide, including a ditch

spruce fence 150cm (5ft) high and 275cm (9ft) wide, including a ditch

Central enclosure

gorse fence 140cm (4½ft) high and 90cm (3ft) wide

spruce fence 140cm (4½ft) high and 90cm (3ft) wide

◄ The Chair: 155cm (5ft 2in) high and 295cm (9ft 8in) wide, including a ditch. Jockeys say it is the most difficult jump. It's been described as an opening like an enormous mouth, waiting to take you into it.

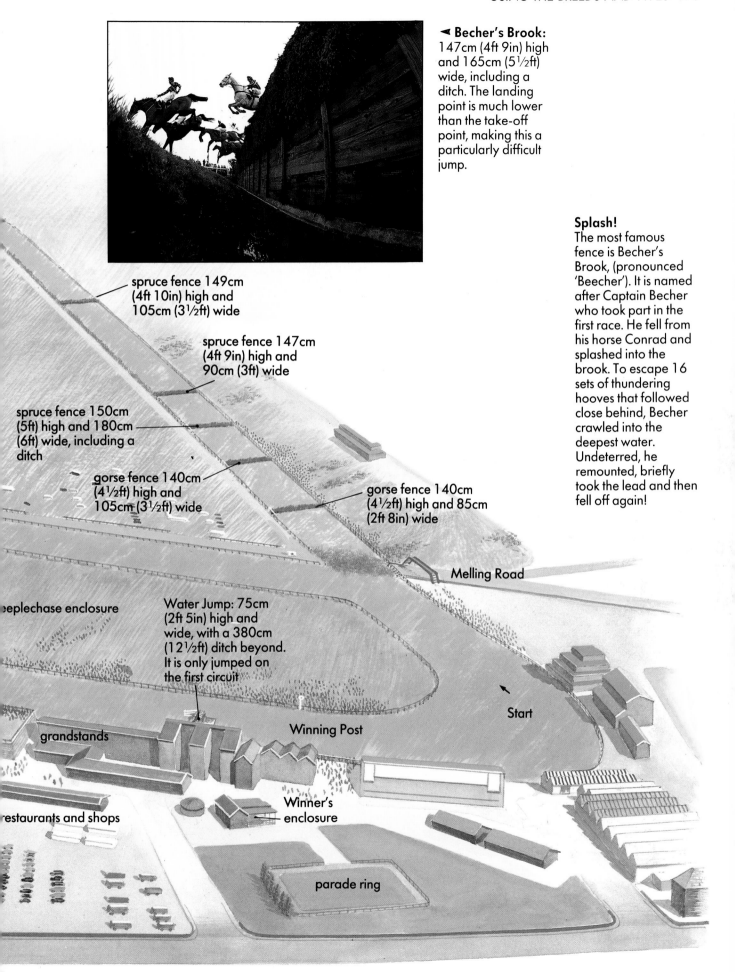

◄ **Becher's Brook:**
147cm (4ft 9in) high and 165cm (5½ft) wide, including a ditch. The landing point is much lower than the take-off point, making this a particularly difficult jump.

**Splash!**
The most famous fence is Becher's Brook, (pronounced 'Beecher'). It is named after Captain Becher who took part in the first race. He fell from his horse Conrad and splashed into the brook. To escape 16 sets of thundering hooves that followed close behind, Becher crawled into the deepest water. Undeterred, he remounted, briefly took the lead and then fell off again!

spruce fence 149cm (4ft 10in) high and 105cm (3½ft) wide

spruce fence 147cm (4ft 9in) high and 90cm (3ft) wide

spruce fence 150cm (5ft) high and 180cm (6ft) wide, including a ditch

gorse fence 140cm (4½ft) high and 105cm (3½ft) wide

gorse fence 140cm (4½ft) high and 85cm (2ft 8in) wide

Melling Road

eeplechase enclosure

Water Jump: 75cm (2ft 5in) high and wide, with a 380cm (12½ft) ditch beyond. It is only jumped on the first circuit

Start

grandstands

Winning Post

restaurants and shops

Winner's enclosure

parade ring

# Russian steps

Many of the Russian breeds are used in troikas, spectacular three-horse sledges or carriages which were designed to combine grace with speed.

## Harmony and elegance

As well as being an elegant way to get about, travelling in a troika has a driving style of its own.

Three horses are harnessed in a row. The outer (trace) horses are driven at a canter, and are usually ordinary riding horses. The centre horse, however, moves at a very fast trot to keep up, and because of this a specialist trotting breed is always preferred.

Using three horses gave the harness its name, as 'troika' comes from the Russian word for 'three'. It's likely that

◄ **A four-span version** of the troika demands even greater skills from the driver — with the two outer horses having to match their speed to that of the inner pair.

## Dashing through the snow

The thrilling speed of a troika inspired writers and artists. One Russian author wrote: 'Oh horses, what horses! Are whirlwinds hidden in your manes?' And this dramatic illustration appeared in an English magazine in 1877.

the troika was first used in the time of Tsar Peter The Great, who ruled Russia in the late 17th and early 18th century. He started the aristocratic fashion of moving between town and country homes, and noble families used troikas to move all their belongings with a touch of style!

### Training a troika team

Making up a troika requires skill. For best effect, the team of horses should be the same colour. More importantly, they must also be matched for pace and temperament so they move in harmony at speed.

It can take over a year to train a team of horses. The central horse does the main pulling work. It runs between a pair of shafts, as if harnessed for an ordinary single carriage.

The outer horses are linked to the sleigh and to the centre horse – to whom they must adapt their step – by leather straps. Fast travel is the only way to stay warm in the bitter cold of Russian winters, so the driver makes sure they are kept on the move. And plenty of blankets are essential to keep the passengers warm.

◄ **Troika rides are a popular tourist attraction** in Moscow, as are the troika races which are held during the city's Winter Festival in January each year.

◄ **The leather harness** of these perfectly matched Orlov Trotters is decorated with silver studs and tassles. A stirrup-like pouch holds the strap that connects from the collar to the shaft.

### ★ TROTTING POWER

Orlov Trotters are famous Russian horses, named after Count Orlov, the nobleman who first developed the breed in 1777.

Always a popular riding and carriage horse, their qualities of hardiness and courage made the Orlov an excellent choice for pulling troikas.

In later years, these same qualities were chosen for harness racing and, by the end of the 19th century, the Orlov was thought to be the supreme trotting horse.

### JINGLE BELLS

Craftsmen take great pride in the troika's design. The wooden yoke on the centre horse, called a *duga*, is brightly painted and a bell is hung in the middle.

Sometimes more bells of differing sizes and tones hang from the rest of the harness — so you can hear the troika long before you see it!

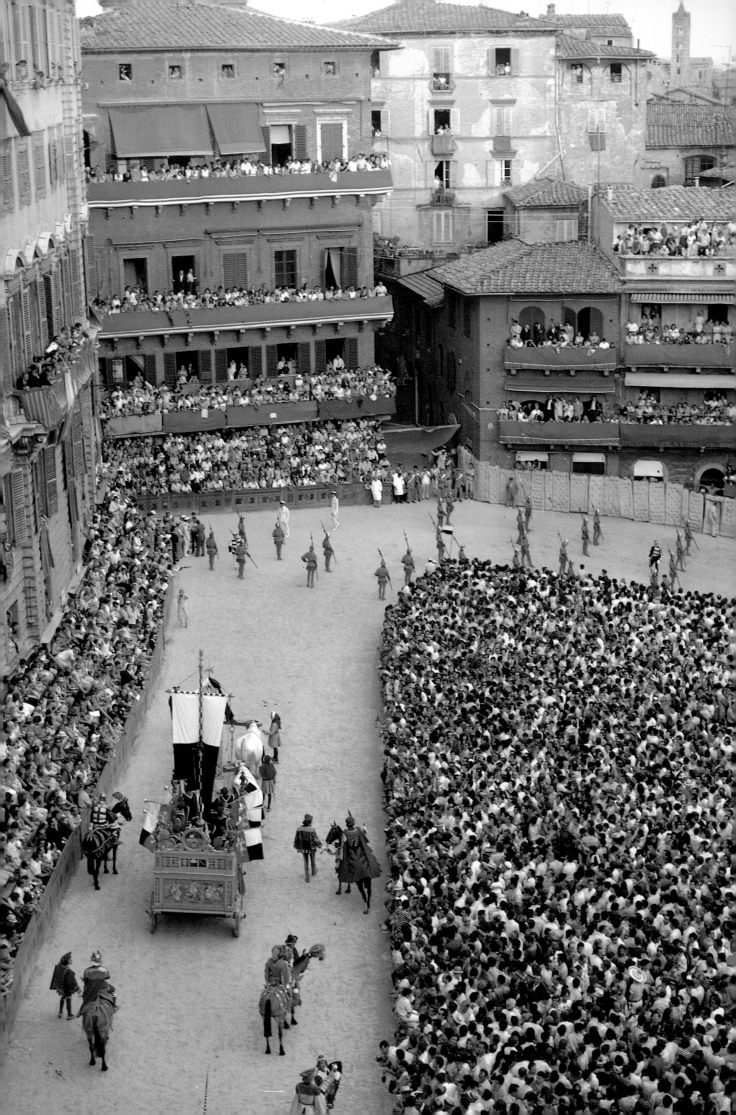

# Sienese whirl

Barbs were the first horses used in the annual horse races known as the *Palio* in the Italian city of Siena. Palio in Italian means 'banner', and a silk banner is the winner's prize.

## Drawing lots

There are two main races each year in Siena: on July 2 and on August 16.

Training for the Palio starts several months ahead. Owners test the staying power of their horses, and the jockeys train in the countryside outside Siena. Before the horses can be chosen to run for the Palio they have to be seen in other public race trials.

Siena has 17 surrounding districts called *contrade* and each contrada hopes to run a horse in the Palio. The race takes place round the ancient city square called the *Campo*. But the path has never been widened, and there is only enough room for ten horses to race safely. So just 20 days before the Palio, lots are drawn to decide which districts can take part. Lots also decide which of their horses will run and their place at the starting line.

## The first Palio

The races are thought to be relics of contests held inside and outside the city since mediaeval times. The first Palio was run in honour of a visiting Duke, and even today a special Palio is held to mark the visit of a distinguished guest.

Between 1629 and 1667 Prince Mattias dei Medici was Governor of the city of Siena. The Prince had a stable of Barb horses from northern Africa. He admired the breed for its speed and was an enthusiastic follower of the Palio. All the contrade were granted permission to use his horses for the races.

Since mediaeval times each contrada has had its own traditional heraldry colours and emblems. Then, as now, the jockeys rode bareback and wore the colours of the particular contrada that they represented.

## Build-up to the races

The races are steeped in tradition, and there are displays and ceremonies ➤

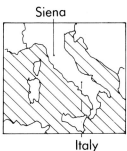

◄ ⋏ **The centre of Siena,** in northern Italy, becomes a sea of colour, as flags are displayed wherever they can be seen.

▼ **Horses** are brought to Siena in good time for the Palio. And one at least will stay on at the victory supper afterwards — the winning horse is guest of honour.

◄ **In the Middle Ages** the Palio was a race ridden on buffaloes! Today oxen still appear — to pull a float that bears the black and white banner of the city, along with the Palio banner awarded to the winners.

## The costumes of Siena

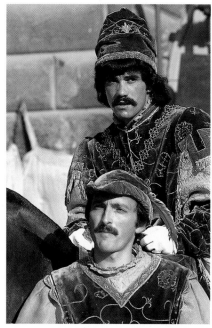

▲ **Each district** (contrada) has its own colours and emblem.

▲ **This horse** displays the panther emblem for its region.

▲ **This drummer** is from the Contrada dell'Oca – the goose!

▲ **Those taking part** in the procession take their seats on a special stand reserved for them. For the public, it's a squash to get a good view.

➤ **The horses must** race three times round the city square – a total length of just under one kilometre (about half a mile).

for several days before the contest itself takes place.

Three days before the Palio is run, the contrade hang their flags in Siena's piazza. Each district competing elects a Captain, and between 11 o'clock and midday on the day of the race Captains present their jockeys to the Mayor and the Palio organizers.

The jockey's name is recorded and, from now on, neither he nor his horse can be substituted. Each contrada taking part holds a church ceremony where horse and rider are blessed.

The people are superstitious. For example, they believe it is a sign of good luck if their horse sheds its droppings inside the church. But a tangle during the flag-waving display on the day is seen as a bad sign.

At three o'clock in the afternoon, the bell in the piazza rings, and a colourful parade begins. The procession of flag-wavers and musicians makes its way though the city to the piazza. A troop of

costumed horsemen trot, then gallop round the race circuit. As the gallop begins, the riders draw their swords and hold them high up in the air.

## Under starter's orders

The race competitors now make their appearance and the prize banner is hoisted up for all to see. A white flag waves from the courtyard of the Town Hall – the signal to fire off a cannon. Two wardens hand out whips to the jockeys and the bugles sound. As the jockeys raise their whips in the air, a steward calls out their starting orders ready for the race.

## The race begins

The rope falls and at last the Palio begins. The horses must gallop round the city square three times. The Palio is as much a jousting event as a race. The rules allow the jockeys to push opponents off their horses with their whips.

The winning jockey raises his whip as he passes the line, and a cannon sounds the end of the race. Amid great excitement, the banner is lowered from the judges' stand and is displayed for days afterwards by the proud contrada.

The winning horse receives a heroic welcome: on the day after the victory, he is paraded through the city in a grand lap of honour.

▲ **Processions** with musicians take up a great part of the day, and add to the build-up of excitement.

The colours here belong to the Contrada Capitana dell'Onda, whose emblem is a sea-wave with dolphin.

★ **THE EMBLEMS**
The 17 districts each have an emblem displayed on their costumes. They are:
☐ Eagle
☐ Snail
☐ Sea-wave with dolphin
☐ Panther
☐ Forest with rhinoceros
☐ Tortoise
☐ Owl
☐ Unicorn
☐ Shell
☐ Tower and elephant
☐ Ram
☐ Caterpillar
☐ Dragon
☐ Giraffe
☐ Porcupine
☐ Wolf
☐ Goose

# An American dream

The Kentucky Horse Park was created in 1976 as a showpiece for breeds of horse from all over the world. The park is a popular attraction for horse-lovers, and with plenty to see, it is like an equestrian version of Disneyland. It covers an area of some 1500 acres and the entire park is surrounded by traditional Kentucky post and rail fencing in the true local style.

## Blue look

For most Kentuckians, horses are a first love. Kentucky is the heart of the American racehorse breeding industry, and is known as 'blue grass' country. Kentucky grass really is blue. It takes on a bluish tinge in certain light and at particular times of the year. Horses thrive on it because it is high quality.

Lexington in Kentucky is where most of the major Thoroughbred racehorse

▼ **The Missouri Foxtrotter** is one of the 30 breeds kept at the park. It is a pacing horse whose smooth gait is said to resemble the steps of a Foxtrot dance.

studs are based. Here, horses with magical names such as Danzig and Storm Cat stand at stud. Their offspring are sold for millions of dollars at the horse sales each summer.

## In the public eye

Visitors used to flock to these studs to see the stallions, but many have closed their gates to the public to protect the horses, and to allow the day's routine to continue uninterrupted. The park was created so that people could continue to enjoy seeing fine horses.

Local breeders now lend their horses to the park. There is a small team of full-time stable staff, but the park also acts as a training centre. Young students in horsy jobs gain practical experience by working there.

## Sport and work

For the visitor, there are exhibition halls that display every aspect of the horse world. One museum explains how the ancestors of the horse lived in prehistoric times. Any question about the different breeds of horse today can be put to a giant computer that displays the answers on a giant screen.

Examples of equestrian sports can be seen in the Horse in Sport Hall, together with the different kinds of tack and equipment used. You can also see the largest stable yard in the world, and a miniature layout of a typical stud – Kentucky-style!

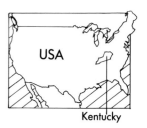

▲ The blue-grass country of Kentucky has proved ideal for rearing horses.

▼ New Zealand's Carol Harrison and Topic compete in a World Championship three-day event at the park.

►**A parade** is held twice a day in the main arena. This Mustang is one of the 30 different types of horse staying at the park at one time. The parade is the only chance for visitors to see them all together.

▼**'Cowboys'** on Pintos act as stewards and are on hand to guide visitors to the exhibitions they want to see.

◄**The American Shetland** takes its place in the parade. The breed bears little resemblance to the British Shetland. It has a high-stepping action, similar to the Hackney pony.

▼ **A Peruvian Paso Fino** mare and foal stop to greet visitors to their field.

# Trotting races in St Moritz

**▲ The famous Alps** and the frozen lake of St Moritz provide a breathtaking setting for exciting winter sports. The horses wear rugs when practising for the trotting races (inset).

**► The racing sleighs** are streamlined for speed. Safety is also important, and to ensure that all competitors meet the strict standards required, the St Moritz Racing Association issues a standard sleigh to each driver.

For Trotters, the most spectacular races are across the frozen St Moritz lake in Switzerland. The lake is on the southern side of the Alps and freezes over in the winter.

## Horse sports on snow

The first trotting race was held in 1906. It took place on roadside tracks and not on the lake because the ice was too thin that year. The lake has to be frozen to at least 46cm (18ins) deep before it is safe enough to race on.

In trotting events, the horses travel at a brisk pace, pulling a driver and sleigh. The sleighs used are specially designed to overcome some of the problems of racing in winter conditions. They are built high off the ground for greater speed. This also helps to shield the driver from the spray of snow kicked up by flying hooves. The sleighs look different from the traditional horse-drawn models that take tourists on sightseeing trips. But, surprisingly, both kinds weigh the same.

## Preparing the winter turf

The lake of St Moritz is 1,856m (6,124ft) above sea level. It is usually not till December that the lake begins to freeze over and becomes covered by a white carpet of snow.

Before the broad race track can be marked out with stakes and rails, the

surface has to be smoothed. In the past, teams of horses dragged rollers across the lake. Sometimes ski students would help out – and even herds of cows!

But times have changed and nowadays the same bulldozer that prepares the ski runs in the area is used to smooth out the lake's race track. Although it is more efficient, clearing the frozen lake like this has its dangers. There have been cases when the ice has given way and the machine has sunk!

## Practice runs

Horses taking part in the race have to get used to pulling a sleigh and rider in a seating position that's different from non-competitive travel. They can practise on local roads, and are allowed to go through their paces on the lake itself just before the race starts.

## Racing techniques on snow

Racing on a snow track is a bit like going over heavy sand, except the snow

is powdery and flies up easily.

There are advantages of snow racing: the track itself is flatter than any other kind of ground and, because it has been well-prepared, trotting at speed over it is very safe. The snow here is powdery and dry, not wet and slippery.

Many horses who run badly on grass tracks compete successfully on the famous St Moritz 'white turf'.

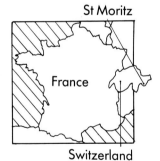

St Moritz

France

Switzerland

### Special racing shoes

▶ **To prevent** hard snow packing in the hooves, winter racing stables used an adapted shoe that had a rubber plate across the sole of the horse's hoof.

▶ **A new design** was developed more recently by a St Moritz blacksmith, with a raised rubber ring. Patches are forged on to help the horse get a firm grip on the powdery 'flying' surface. The shoes are now popular in other countries where winter sports on horseback take place.

◄ **The trotting races** are fast and furious. The drivers sit back with their feet up, and goggles protect their eyes from the flying snow.

# The greatest show of all

Warmbloods are bred to compete and one of the great tests is the Aachen Show in Germany. There is a small show in March, but the main show is in mid-summer – six spectacular days that have been described as Hickstead, Goodwood and the Windsor Driving Trials all rolled into one splendid occasion!

▼ **Competitors** attend by invitation only. Caletto and Dr Michael Rüping are one of the top West German partnerships.

## Top attraction

Competitors know that to win a Grand Prix, or to belong to a team that scoops a Nations Cup, means they have beaten the best in the world.

The show jumping events are the main focus of the week. The huge arena is one of the finest in existence: long before Hickstead was founded in Eng-

land, Aachen had permanent obstacles such as a lake, banks, hedges and water ditches. Show jumping has taken place at Aachen since the 1920s, and the Grand Prix – which was first held in 1927 – is one of the oldest and most difficult competitions to win.

The show has always employed the world's leading course designers, and the fences have a reputation for being big but fair. This, together with the

◄ **Show jumping** takes place in Aachen's main arena. Although the grandstand can accommodate 45,000 spectators, there is never a spare seat, or even standing space, on Grand Prix or Nations Cup day.

▲ **Aachen** is in West Germany, close to the Dutch and Belgian borders.

◄ **Danish dressage champions** Anne Grethe Jensen and Marzog have stolen the limelight in recent years, although in the past, victory often went to Germany's famous Olympic riders.

▲ **Ann Kursinski** is one of the top show jumpers in the USA and in 1991 she represented her country in Aachen riding Star Man.

electric atmosphere created by the huge and knowledgeable crowd, makes jumping at Aachen a special challenge.

## Tough Competition

Competition is also tough for the Nations Cup, where teams of four riders from each country take part. There can be up to 15 teams involved.

In the European Championship, riders compete only on their own horses. But in the World Championship, the four highest-placed riders of three qualifying contests, go forward to a change-horse final. They each have to ride their own horse and then the horses of the other three finalists.

Although the course for this spectacular finale is not nearly as tricky as for the other championships, it is a true test of horsemanship. The riders are given only a few minutes and a couple of

▲ **Nick Skelton's Apollo** was also a record-breaker when in 1988 he became the first horse for some 40 years to win the tough Grand Prix a second time.

▲ **Serious jumping** is balanced by a mixture of speed classes and fun events, including a gallop through the lake!

◄ **When the various** Grands Prix have finished and the prizes have been awarded, all the riders assemble in the main arena.

practice jumps to get used to each new mount.

Driving is almost as popular as show jumping and as many as 30,000 people turn out to watch the marathon through the Aachen woods.

There is also a five-day driving Grand Prix for teams of four horses where entrants compete both for individual awards and for the driving Nations Cup. Each country enters three carriages.

## All classes of dressage

The daily dressage competitions are at all levels, from the Prix St Georges and Intermédiare I and II for less experienced horses to the Grand Prix Special for the top internationals.

Germany has a long tradition of producing top dressage riders, and it is always a challenge for overseas competitors to visit Aachen and take on the Germans at their famous home ground.

◄ **The skill** of driving teams is thoroughly tested. The marathon through the Aachen woods challenges the horses' stamina and the control of their driver.

◄ **Back in the arena,** Nanno Hannssen has his team well-collected for the obstacle course.

▼ **There is** a closing ceremony on the last day of the show. As each team enters the arena, a band plays the national anthem of its country. On the final parade, the whole audience gets to its feet, and everyone waves white handkerchiefs in time to the music!

Morocco

Sahara

# Arabian knights

**Barbs and Arabs are used for one of the most spectacular equestrian festivals – the fantasia which is staged on the fringes of the Sahara Desert.**

## What is a fantasia?

A fantasia is a mock battle, performed at celebrations and at various religious festivals throughout the year. Moroccan fantasias are particularly famous. The events are marked by camel races, dancing, side-shows and open air markets but the highlight comes when bands of armed horsemen gallop into sight.

The riders are divided into separate groups each representing local tribes or families and they take great pride in demonstrating the unity of their 'team' and the skill of their riding. Although the groups are not in direct competition, their performance is taken very seriously: poor riding from one member of a group is a bad reflection on all of them.

## Putting on a show

The rich trappings of gold thread and silk chosen to decorate the horses are a traditional part of the show and the design of the saddles, bridles and stirrups has remained unchanged over hundreds of years. The horses themselves are of Arab or Barb ancestry.

The fantasia takes place within a rectangular arena, flanked by spectators and headed by tents sheltering local dignitaries. The horsemen gallop flat out along the dusty ground – seemingly intent on charging into the tented area. Then, at a signal from their leader, the riders stand up in their stirrups and fire their rifles into the air. The shots mark the end of the display, though the groups take turns to repeat the show throughout the event.

## Royal connections

King Hassan of Morocco is a great enthusiast of fantasias and the displays have flourished in his country since he came to the throne in 1961. A big festival devoted only to fantasia competitions takes place on the second Wednesday of September every year in the Moroccan city of Meknes.

▲ **Moroccan horsemen** ride in thin-soled boots so their stirrup irons are large enough to protect the whole foot.

◄ **Barb horses** from this region are ridden in the fantasias. The guns are made by local craftsmen.

▼ **Musicians** lead the horses to the start of the races. Riders show off their skills by standing on their saddles.

◄ **Fantasias** usually take place in the afternoon as this is the cooler part of the day. They can form part of wedding and other social ceremonies, as well as religious events.

Pictured is a fantasia at a small religious festival near the town of Rabat in Morocco.

▼ **When the team leader** gives the signal, the horsemen must shoot in the air all at the same time. The horses are then brought to an abrupt halt.

➤ **The horse** is honoured in Arab culture and it is believed to be the holiest of all animals. A horse's colour is traditionally significant.

White is the most noted colour for a horse and is associated with men of importance.

Red chestnut horses are thought to be the fastest, and blue roans the most difficult to manage. In some regions, too, black horses are said to be the luckiest.

# Calgary Stampede

Quarter Horses, Palominos and Canadian Cutting Horses are some of the horses used when the cowboys of the 'Wild West' test their bravery and skill in the rough and rugged events of Canada's Calgary Stampede.

## Roping and riding skills

The atmosphere is electric as horse and rider compete in events ranging from acrobatic riding to steer wrestling. Cowboys developed roping and riding skills for daily work, whether it was to master a difficult horse, or to lasso a calf. The name 'rodeo' comes from the Spanish word for round-up, and rodeo events were simply a showy display of everyday work skills.

## Rebel horses

Bucking horses are rebels that have either soured under the saddle, or are born with an untameable instinct and simply don't want to be ridden. Horses

▼ **In the** Saddle Bronc Riding event, the cowboy must stay in the saddle for eight seconds. Another rider on a tame horse gives the cowboy a ride back at the end of his turn.

▲ **Steer wrestling** is risky but spectacular! Quarter Back horses are often used for rodeo events as they are fast and react quickly.

like these are rare to find. They are not taught to buck, but react to humans by being unruly and difficult.

Rodeo stock contractors travel round the country paying thousands of dollars for good bucking horses. For their investment, they make sure their prize stock is well looked after.

## Professional cowboys

Rodeo is a refined sport and, at the highest level, professional cowboys can earn their living from prize money. The main events at the Stampede are the 'big five': saddle bronc riding, bareback riding, calf roping, steer wrestling and bull riding. Four elimination rounds take place over ten days and the top four contestants go on to the final where each cowboy can hope to win the grand prize.

Companies and private sponsors donate the prize money to make sure that the tradition of North American horsemen and horsemanship is kept going.

▲ **Calgary** is ideal for the Stampede as it is in the heart of ranching country.

▲ **In the** Chuck Wagon Race there are four out-riders for each wagon. To win, the whole team must cross the finishing line at the same time. Wagons like these were used in Wild West days to bring the cowboys food when they were out on cattle round-ups.

➤ **Stunt riders** push balancing skills to the limit. The horses are trained to gallop at a steady pace.

## Rules of rodeo

Saddle bronc riding is the classic rodeo event. The horse is saddled and a plain halter is put on with a single rope rein attached. As the horse leaves the enclosed starting pen (chute), a strap tied round the flank is tightened. Because the animal is not used to it, he will buck harder to get rid of it.

The strap is like having a belt snug round you, and does not hurt the horse. Officers from the Society of Prevention of Cruelty to Animals stand by to make sure the horses are well treated.

The cowboys ride with blunt spurs and leather chaps. Rules are strict. Riders are allowed to hold the rope rein, but their other hand must be held up in the air. Competitors are disqualified if their spurs are over the horse's shoulder as the gate opens, and they can only touch the horse when it leaves the chute. If the rider loses a stirrup, is bucked off, or touches any part of the horse or tack with his free hand he can also be eliminated.

For bareback riding, the second most popular event, a double-thick leather pad called a 'rigging' is strapped on the bronc's back and no stirrups or reins are used! Riders hold on to a leather hand-hold near the withers.

## Women's event

The most breathtaking event in rodeo is the only event women can take part in – the barrel race. Horse and rider race round three barrels set in a triangle. They must lean the horses into every barrel turn, almost touching the ground before they race the length of the arena to the next.

Precision is as important as speed because if a barrel is knocked over it adds five seconds' penalty time.

## Prizes awarded

Two top awards are presented at the end of the Stampede: the All-Around Championship is given to the cowboy who has competed in at least two of the five major events, and has won the most prize money in the first three rounds.

Another award is named after Guy Weadick, the American trick roper who founded the Stampede in Calgary back in 1912. This prize is given to the rider who combines outstanding performance with personality and sportsmanship.

◄ **Extra girth straps** and a breastplate keep the Western saddle firmly in place. Fetlock boots protect the horse's legs. The riders wear blue jeans, first designed as tough working clothes for the cattle ranchers. All wear the famous cowboy hats.

▼ **The wild broncos** are brought into the spectator's arena at the opening of the Stampede, and run a circuit of the track.

# Harmony and horsemanship

Lipizzaner stallions perform daily 'horse ballets' to classical music at the Spanish Riding School in Austria's capital – Vienna. The art of high-school riding has been strictly maintained here for 400 years and, each year, the horses travel around the world to share their magic with a wider audience.

## The Spanish Riding School

It may seem confusing that the Spanish Riding School performs in Vienna. But the name is based on tradition; the school takes only Lipizzaner stallions – horses of Spanish origin. In all, they have 70 stallions but at least 25 of these may be abroad taking part in special 'travelling' shows.

## The training

The trained movements are taught gradually and in stages, but the schooling is vigorous and demanding for both the horse and rider. Above all, the trainer must be patient and be familiar with the personality and temperament of each Lipizzaner.

The aim of the training is to make the horse very supple, manoeuvrable and willing to obey the rider's lightest aids. The exercises are based on natural movements but it needs hard work to make the horses equally responsive 'on demand'. Training begins when a stallion is three, and it takes another three years of intensive schooling before a horse is ready to participate in any of the formal displays.

## Schools on the Ground

All the stallions have to learn a number of basic movements (known as 'Schools on the Ground'). The most advanced of these movements on the ground are the *Piaffe* and *Passage* and the *Canter Pirouettes*.

**The Piaffe** is a rhythmical trot on the spot. The aim is for the horse to keep trotting without moving forward and this is very difficult as the horse must be powerful but relaxed.

**The Passage** is another variation of the trot. The horse does move forward in this, but with shorter, higher and more springy steps than in the normal trot. It is spectacular to watch.

**The Pirouette** entails the horse cantering in such a tiny circle that the hind legs stay almost on the same spot.

## Between the pillars

Another exercise is based on work between two pillars. These are round posts sunk into the ground at a distance of 1.5m (5ft) from each other.

Exercising between the pillars helps to strengthen the horse's muscles, especially his hindquarters, and limbers him up to make his joints as supple and flexible as possible.

## Schools above the Ground

Although all the horses come from noble stock and have been specially bred to be strong and intelligent, there are more difficult movements that are only performed by some of the riders and horses. Not all are capable of perfecting the necessary skills, and those selected for training must be even more talented ▶

▲ **The sequences** are precise and difficult to achieve, but look effortless when they are performed.

◀ **The Lipizzaner** shows are still performed in the elegant riding hall built in Vienna, capital of Austria, in 1572. It is the only riding hall of its kind in the world. The sequence pictured here is the standard finale, called the Quadrille and performed by eight stallions.

and athletic than the other horses.

These special exercises are called 'Schools above the Ground' and, like all other displays at Vienna, are based on classical horsemanship. The movements require the horse to balance on his hindquarters with the forelegs lifted.

**In the Pesade** the horse raises his forelegs so that his body is at an angle of 45°. Less than this is a Levade.

**The Courbette** begins in the same way as a Pesade. The stallion must then take several jumps forward, but his forelegs must stay in the air and not touch the ground at any time.

## Individual attention

As each stallion begins his schooling, the expert trainers give him individual attention. They can tell straight away

▼ **The horses** travel round the world to put on their displays, and attract attention wherever they go. Here they are being led through the city of Arles in France.

► **At the stadium** in Arles, the horses limber up before they begin practising for their performance.

how talented the horse is likely to be.

If a Lipizzaner looks suitable for Schools above the Ground, he has a different kind of training from the others. But all the stallions are assessed regularly and each is given the kind of exercises which suit him. The Spanish Riding School recognizes that a horse gives his best performance when he is relaxed and happy.

◄ **Horse and rider** form a bond of friendship as a result of working together so closely.

▼ **Each bridle** bears the crest of the Spanish Riding School.

▼ **Great concentration** is needed to perform the Courbette, as the Lipizzaner stallion has to balance himself perfectly. Long and careful training helps to achieve this difficult series of steps.

# Index

## ACKNOWLEDGEMENTS

**Photographers:** 1 Bob Langrish, 2-3 TSI, 4-5 SW/E, 6-7 TSI, 9(l) Survival Anglia, 9(r) Frank Lane Picture Library, 10 Aquila, 11(tr) Coleman, 11(b) Aquila, 12-13 Zefa, 16(t) Kit Houghton, 16(b) SW/E, 17 SW/E, 18(t) NHPA, 18(b) TSI, 19(l) AP, 19(r) AGE Fotostock, 22-23(t) Survival Anglia, 22-23(b) SW/E, 24(t) Zefa, 24(b) Kit Houghton, 25(t) NHPA, 25(b) Aquila, 26(t) SW/E, 26(b) AP, 27(tr) Kit Houghton, 27(bl) Nordling Horse Breeding Association, 27(br) Bob Langrish, 28 Kit Houghton, 29 AP, 30 Bob Langrish, 31 SW/E, 32(t) Elisabeth Weiland, 32(c) AP, 32(b) Coleman, 33-35 AP, 40-41 Bob Langrish, 42 Coleman, 43 Kit Houghton, 44 NHPA, 45-46 Bob Langrish, 47-48 Kit Houghton, 49 Elisabeth Weiland, 50 Kit Houghton, 51-52 AP, 53 NHPA, 54 Spectrum, 55 Aquila, 56 AP, 57 SW/E, 58 AP, 59-61 Bob Langrish, 62 Coleman, 63-64 AP, 65 Aquila, 66 Kit Houghton, 67 AP, 68 Kit Houghton, 69 AP, 70 Aquila, 71-73 AP, 74 SW/E, 75-78 AP, 79 Kit Houghton, 80 AP, 81 Nature Photographers, 82 (main) Kit Houghton, 82(inset) Bob Langrish, 83(main) Aquila, 83(inset) Bob Langrish, 84-85 AP, 86 Okapia, 87 AP, 88 Aquila, 89 Elisabeth Weiland, 90(c)

Elisabeth Weiland, 90(b) AP, 91-92 AP, 93 NHPA, 94-96 AP, 97 Explorer, 98 AP, 99-100 Kit Houghton, 101 (main) AP, 101 (inset) Explorer, 102-3 AP, 105 Bruce Coleman, 106(main) Elisabeth Weiland, 106(inset) Bob Langrish, 107 Coleman, 108-9 AP, 110 Kit Houghton, 111 Elisabeth Weiland, 112 AP, 113 Bob Langrish, 114 Mike Roberts, 115-119 AP, 120 Elisabeth Weiland, 121 Coleman, 122 Jacana, 123-4 AP, 125 SW/E, 126-7 AP, 128-9 SW/E, 130(main) AP, 130(inset) Kit Houghton, 131-2 AP, 133 Kit Houghton, 134-5 TSI, 136 Kit Houghton, 137 AP, 138-9 SW/E, 140 Aquila, 141 AP, 142 Coleman, 143-146 AP, 147 Kit Houghton, 148-157 AP, 158-159 Steven Somerville/Eaglemoss, 160 NHPA, 161-2 J.Allan Cash, 162-3 NHPA, 164(t) Bob Langrish, 164(b) SW/E, 165-6 Hutchison Library, 166 Robert Harding Picture Library, 167 Hutchison, 168-9 TSI, 170(t) Mary Evans Picture Library, 170(c) Mike Roberts, 170-1 Mike Roberts, 171(t) AP, 171(c) AllSport, 171(b) Kit Houghton, 172-3 Sporting Pictures, 174(t) AP, 174-5 Fotokhronika, 175 Mary Evans Picture Library, 176-7 AP, 178 Robert Harding Picture Library, 179(t) J.Allan Cash,

179(b) Hutchison Library, 180(tl,tc) Grazia Neri, 180(tr) J.Allan Cash, 180(bl) Robert Harding Picture Library, 180-1 Azienda Autonoma Turismo, Siena, 181(t) J.Allan Cash, 182-5 Kit Houghton, 186-7 Bob Langrish, 186(b) Mike Roberts, 186-7 Mike Roberts, 187(b) Bob Langrish, 188-9 TSI, 190 Elisabeth Weiland, 191(t) Kit Houghton, 191(b) Elisabeth Weiland, 192(tl) Elisabeth Weiland, 192(c) Bob Langrish, 192(b) Elisabeth Weiland, 193(t) Bob Langrish, 193(c,b) Elisabeth Weiland, 194 Kit Houghton, 195(t) Explorer, 195(b) Frank Spooner Pictures, 196-197 Explorer, 198-9 TSI, 198(inset) Bob Langrish, 200 Bob Langrish, 201(t) Alastair Scott, 201(b) Explorer, 202 Peter Roberts, 203-205 Frank Spooner Library, 205(b) Peter Roberts.
**Illustrators:** 14-15 Denys Ovenden; 20-21, 36-37, 38-39 John Thompson/Garden Studios.

## Key
AP – Animal Photography
Coleman – Bruce Coleman Photo Library
SW/E – Shona Wood/Eaglemoss
TSI – Tony Stone Images